The Energizing
 Heart

Experience Increased Energy
by Harnessing the Power of your Heart.

The Energizing  Heart

Experience Increased Energy
by Harnessing the Power of your Heart.

Nathalie Campeau, M.D.

You Are Energy, Inc.
Fort Lauderdale, FL

The Energizing Heart
Nathalie Campeau, MD

First published in the United States in 2005 by You Are Energy, Inc.

Copyright © 2005 Nathalie Campeau

All rights reserved. No part of this book can be reproduced or transmitted in any form or by any means, electronic or mechanical, including photocopying, recording, or by any information retrieval system without prior permission in writing of the author.

The information offered in this book were gleaned by the author and based on her personal experience. They are presented here in good faith as an invitation to use ones heart to increase personal energy. It is up to the reader to criticize, read alternative opinions and come to an independent view. The author rejects any responsibility for any decisions about life, diet, or exercise plan. Any action taken after reading the material here enclosed is solely the reader's responsibility. The reader is recommended to form his or her own opinion on these matters after reading widely and consulting appropriate professionals. The author does not dispense medical advice or prescribe the use of any technique as a form of treatment for medical problems, either directly or indirectly. The reader is encouraged to get medical advice from his or her personal physician. The intent of the author is only to offer information of a general nature to indicate options for better personal energy management.

ISBN 0-9761172-0-7

Library of Congress Control Number: 2004096912

Library of Congress Cataloging-in-Publication Data:
Campeau, Nathalie, 1950-
The Energizing Heart: Increase your Energy by Harnessing the Power of your Heart.
Includes bibliographical references and index.

Printed in China

Distributed in the United States by
You Are Energy, Inc.
PO Box 8221
Fort Lauderdale, FL 33310

You Are Energy, Inc.
Fort Lauderdale, FL
www.YouAreEnergy.com

Dedication

To all those whose loving hearts

allowed me to bloom.

Thank you from the bottom of my heart.

Acknowledgments

This book would not have been possible without the cheering support of my mother, Fernande Campeau, my brother Jean, my sister Johanne, and all my family. I also want to thank my brother-in-law, Michel Chripounoff, who was instrumental in shaping this "Energizing Heart" project by sharing an article mentioning Dr. Servan-Schreiber's work on cardiac coherence.

Special thanks to my very talented friends Gary Walker, who splendidly edited this manuscript, and Ray Yang, whose fabulous pictures of smiling faces are included in this book. Special thanks also to my cousins Ian and Ann for sharing with us the pictures of their adorable children.

I am very grateful for the unconditional support of my friends, Madeleine Duhaime and Vincent Julson who had the patience to proof read the manuscripts. I wish to extend my gratitude to Christine Coil, Daniel Forest, Elisabeth Rossen, and want to mention the support of Reverends Jim Lockard, Arleen Bump and Ernie Chu of the Fort Lauderdale Religious Science Center.

I am eternally thankful to my dance teachers, world championsBilly Fajardo and Katie Marlow, who greatly contributed to increasing my stamina and passion for dancing, and, consequently, my global level of energy.

My dentists, Dr. Larry and Maxine Sindledecker, have contributed with their professional and exceptional artistic skills to the radiance of my smile.

Last but not least, I want to give special thanks to John Cattlley at Globallink Production Solutions whose dedication made the production of this book possible.

Table of Contents

Introduction   8

SECTION 1: THE HEART: OUR NEWEST FRONTIER   15

Chapter 1: The Personal Energy Crisis   16

Chapter 2: Heart –Brain Synchronization   28

Chapter 3: Cardiac Coherence   44

SECTION 2: HEART-SMILING   59

Chapter 4: Heart-Smiling   60

Chapter 5: Physiology and Function of a Smile   72

SECTION 3: APPLICATIONS OF HEART-SMILING TO PERSONAL ENERGY MANAGEMENT   89

Chapter 6: Seven Levels of Personal Energy   90

Chapter 7: What is Energy?   136

Chapter 8: Discover your Energy Type   154

Chapter 9: Taking Charge of your Energy   178

Conclusion: Engaging your Heart   196

Table of Heat-Smiling Applications   200

Index   201

References   203

Introduction

"Doctor, I don't have any energy!"

I practiced medicine for almost twenty years and heard this complaint from thousands of patients. Patients of all ages saying, *"Doctor, I don't have any energy!"* Patients from all socioeconomic backgrounds and nationalities would come to me with the same problem. They were living in an energy slump, hoping I could make a difference.

Energy deficiency is a symptom that can be attributed to many different phenomenons. Various acute and chronic physical conditions are accompanied by fatigue: diabetes, heart diseases, cancers, and anemia, to name only a few. Lethargic energy levels often alert medical professionals to the possibility of mental conditions such as depression, chronic anxiety and stress related disorders.

My work as a physician was to diagnose and treat those physical and emotional problems. However, in many cases, after a thorough examination and investigation, no medical problem could be identified to explain the lack of energy. This was always very disappointing and frustrating for both the patient and myself. Very often I had to admit my powerlessness in treating this symptom.

In my practice I saw that many times, energy depletion had very little to do with a medical condition. Chronic fatigue was more often linked to painful relationships. People were being energy depleted from circumstances either at home with a spouse, a child or a parent, or at work with a coworker or an employer.

Lack of energy, at other times, was caused by a lack of passion in the patient's life, a lack of drive or purposefulness. Some cases of energy shortage were associated with a pessimistic or cynical view of life, which deprived these persons from the capacity to hope for and enjoy a happy existence. In the end, it does not matter whether the cause of fatigue is physical, mental or spiritual; lack of energy is always a very debilitating quality-of-life factor for those who experience it.

Western medicine is most efficient in acute situations, those where the advances of pharmacotherapy and new computerized-imaging-enhanced surgery are saving lives every day. However, for chronic disease, the results are very limited because of the limits of western medicine to efficiently deal with energy deficiencies. For these reasons, I decided to investigate energy management systems and research alternatives.

Increasing my own Personal Energy

We are all born with curious minds hungering to learn. Some people are like me and thrive on learning more about science, how the world functions and how the human body works. With an undergraduate degree in biochemistry, a doctorate in medicine and my love for brain functioning, it was an easy jump into the relatively new field of Addiction Medicine; an enjoyable, challenging and immensely gratifying new area of medicine.

I am an avid reader, fodder to an insatiable intellectual appetite. Many authors have been my greatest teachers in fields like science, philosophy and metaphysics. One in particular, was Ralph Waldo Emerson. In his famous inspiring essay "Self-Reliance"[2], he exhorts us to think by ourselves and not let authorities dictate what should be held as truth. I still identify with this "rebellious mindset" today. I like doing my own thinking and having the option of choosing what is right for me on my own. I never buy into mainstream ideas without investigation.

We all should reassess the 'normal' and never comply in order to adapt to what others may call the 'real' world. Values and codes of ethics must never become dogma. Organized religious groups and political parties are often inflexible institutions with a fixed set of codes; they usually do not welcome in their ranks those who challenge the norms.

We must prioritize our lives according to what matters to us, not to what is important to some outside authority. From time to time, we need to start going through the process of identifying the values that drive us and re-prioritize our lives accordingly. Soul-searching is a very private endeavor; a never-ending quest which leads to personal answers, personal truth and personal meaning.

Western Medicine has lost its fascination. It has become too restrictive as if it were wearing a coat that it had outgrown. Caring is no longer valued in the health industry. Moreover, an ineffective decision making process totally excludes caregiver input. People with no medical training and no concern for patient needs are pressuring policy makers into making many important treatment decisions; like the length of time a patient is allowed to stay in the hospital, for instance. The big winners in the health industry are the shareholders of medical service companies or pharmaceutical companies. The biggest losers are the patients.

Institutions will never be changed from within. New tools must be researched outside conservative circles of western medicine and political power in order to find ways to improve the quality of healthcare. Researchers must look for solutions down paths less traveled. There are many optimistic physicians who believe that "there must be a better way" and there must be an answer to energy depletion.

Most physicians are already suggesting complementary approaches to conventional medical practices to their patients. New therapeutic options, especially those tested under rigorous research protocol, are considered and recommended more everyday. In cases of many chronic diseases where western medicine has demonstrated limited results, alternative techniques have been shown to be very helpful adjuvant treatments.

Medical training has been aimed at treating diseases and alleviating symptoms. However, health is much more than the absence of disease. Doctors are trained to make a sick person symptom-free and not to bring a symptom-free person to a state of radiant health. **But, it is radiant health that patients deserve!** New tools have to be found for managing personal energy, tools that will help people reach this very real state of radiant health.

Information is being gathered from various fields concerned with some aspect of energy, like quantum physics, cosmology's dark matter and dark energy, the new neurosciences and oriental theories about "Qi" energy . Recent developments in understanding what consciousness is and how it works and metaphysical studies of that which lies beyond the physical world are being meticulously perused and contemplated.

The field of Energy Medicine has emerged.

Energy medicine is based on the premises that our physical bodies possess an intangible energy field, and that problems at the physical level need to be corrected at the energy level. Traditional oriental medicine is based on this approach. In the West, we are beginning to familiarize ourselves with energy-based techniques like acupuncture and 'therapeutic touch'.

Meditation has also become a popular stress management technique, which enhances personal energy quality. Many studies have shown the benefits of regular meditation in reducing stress related illnesses. However, people and doctors still resist using meditation techniques because of the time factor involved and the need for a quiet solitary place to practice. Meditation can take 20 to 30 minutes in a quiet place on a daily basis to practice

In the 90's, discoveries in neuroscience paved the way to new understandings of brain functioning and the respective roles of the emotional brain and the intellect. During this same period, Daniel Goleman introduced the notion of EQ: Emotional Intelligence. The clinical applications of Emotional Intelligence concepts have been developed to foster better integration of intellect and emotion in order to promote a fuller life experience.

More recent research has shown that the heart has its own intelligence and can communicate and influence the brain and other organs. Research in the area of the heart-brain connection has thrown light onto the benefits of "cardiac coherence", a physical state where brain and heart work in synchronicity to help balance all bodily function.

With personal energy as a challenge, the importance of applying this new knowledge of proven scientific concepts to the area of health and energy management has become undeniable. This book presents the findings of my research on personal energy management and hopes to enlighten and familiarize you with the latest techniques I have gleaned from various areas of study. The techniques presented here offer tremendous possibilities for healthier lives, regained energy and personal transformation.

The study of the heart is a new frontier. The latest research in this area reexplores the heart's role in the human experience and the consequential implications for human potential development. These scientific discoveries are shared in the first part of this book: *"The Heart, a New Frontier"*.

The second part is entitled *"Heart-Smiling"* and describes a simple but powerful technique that uses energy generated by the heart to influence and modulate cerebral activity.

The third section of this book, *"Applications of 'Heart-Smiling' in Personal Energy Management"*, identifies different applications of heart-brain synchronization in everyday life. Because "Heart-Smiling" is effective at transforming perceptions and attitudes, it can be successfully used to manage personal energy.

People who have used cardiac coherence techniques report increased energy and enhanced quality of life in the areas of health, work and relationships.

These new scientific findings have the potential to tremendously impact your life. When people learn to willfully engage their heart, they can transform their experience of any situation into harmonious energy flow.

In offering you the energizing technique of "Heart-Smiling", I join the ranks of many physicians who recommend complementary medical approaches for augmenting the well being of their patients. Doctors like Deepak Chopra, Bernie Siegel, Andrew Weil, David Servan-Schreiber and Dean Ornish are all pioneers in the field of global medicine and ardent proselytes of radiant health.

I sincerely hope that by learning to connect your brain with your heart, you will not only improve your energy levels but the quality of your life, your family's and your community's.

I invite you now to use "Heart-Smiling" to access the amazing source of energy in your own heart. In your heart lies the power of love, compassion, and gratitude. Using this technique will help you come to the realization that you are "Love-powered".

Take an active part in the evolution of the human race by bringing the higher energies of your heart into play and live from a place of understanding, appreciation and cooperation. The world desperately needs your heartfelt smiles. Give generously!

Nathalie Campeau, MD
Fort Lauderdale, 2004.

Section 1

The Heart:
Our Newest Frontier

The Heart: Our Newest Frontier

Chapter 1

The Personal Energy Crisis

Look around. How many of your relatives, friends and coworkers are always on the run, exhausted, irritable, depressed or cynical? Who do you see who would benefit from an energy boost?

What about you? Are you trapped in a "black hole" where your precious energy is drained and seems out of reach? What would your life be if you had more energy? Are there activities you never do because you are too tired? Would you play golf, scuba dive, or ski if you had the energy? Would you decorate your house, exercise more, write a book? Would you spend more time with your family? Would you get involved in your community? If you were not exhausted after work, you could use your evening to have fun and enjoy yourself. Imagine waking up every day with loads of energy? Imagine not having to spend your weekends or vacations recuperating!

Today's *personal energy crisis* is the worst energy crisis that the world has ever known. It has affected everyone! Our single most important natural resource on the planet, human capital, is tired out. People in wealthier countries, are exhausted because they cannot afford to take the time to recharge. In underdeveloped countries, the lack of clean water, food and medication drains weak bodies and produces apathetic minds.

The Personal Energy Crisis

Having energy is like having electricity: it is when you are out of it that you value it most.

Chronic lack of energy is increasingly rampant around the globe. Advanced technologies that promised less working hours and more leisure time did not deliver. But, on the contrary, the demands that the workplace puts on individuals today, often with little satisfaction or security in return, has brought about an era of implacable performance and merciless stress. The stress factor is the new number one cause of illness and death in our "civilized" world[3].

In western civilizations, statistics on drug use "helping" people cope with the stress of modern living are shocking. The list[4] of the twenty best selling drugs in America and Europe includes nerve pills, sleeping pills, mood altering drugs, or pills to counteract the effect of stress on the stomach, the heart, arteries and other organs.

Fatigue, the modern plague, is only temporarily and partially relieved by occidental medicine, which is more effective at treating acute problems like infections or surgical conditions. Even "natural" medicine has its limitations in this area. There does not seem to be an easy universal solution. How should this enormous hindrance be addressed? Is there a way to avoid constantly running on an empty tank? Can we replenish personal energy?

Fortunately, most causes of energy problems are preventable and personal energy management can be learned. This chapter covers the different aspects of energy and the principles of personal energy management that can be practiced in order to enjoy a life worth living.

Personal Energy Management

Doctors hear, "I don't have any energy", over and over. It is a haunting complaint, which has fueled present day physicians to research new methods that could bring a permanent solution to this chronic socio-energetic problem.

It has become more and more evident that medical science has very little effective long-term solutions for chronic energy depletion. For this reason, the area of energy deficiency surged to the fore in medical research. Everyone wants to learn more about human energy. What this energy is, where it comes from, how it is produced and how one increases his or her charge of this vital life-sustaining substance?

My experiences in the area of addiction medicine interested me in developing a model for personal energy management. Addicts are perfect examples of walking "black holes". They are exhausted, frustrated, depressed and very often feel hopeless about their future. Working with addicts and their co-dependent spouses, children and parents is a good arena to learn more about energy on all levels: what drains energy and what produces energy.

Co-dependents are people who are emotionally involved with alcoholics and addicts and accomplices in energy drain. Just like addicts, they need to learn to manage their own energy and not to waste it on emotional games that leave everyone empty and depressed.

Four Aspects of Energy

As individuals, we experience elevated levels of personal energy as feelings of well-being and optimism. Feeling energized and powerful is a wonderful experience. Those wanting to feel an abundance of energy as often as possible have discovered that the secret to sustaining energy lies in ones ability to manage it, learn to replenish it and avoid getting leaks.

Optimal levels of vibrant personal energy springs from the simultaneous balancing of four aspects of the human experience; physical well-being, emotional balance, mental alertness and spiritual realization. These four intimately related elements must be present in perfect equilibrium and totally integrated.

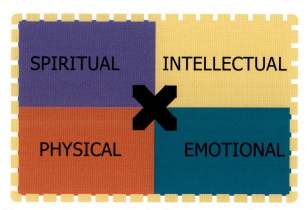

Figure 1: Four aspects of vibrant personal energy

1. Physical energy peaks when we give our body what it needs to function optimally: healthy nutrients, rest, touch and exercise.

2. Emotional energy is optimized when our relationships to others and ourselves are harmonious.

3. **Intellectual energy** is enhanced when continuous learning and constant creating nourish us intellectually, and when we take charge of our thinking and decision-making.

4. **Spiritual energy** gives us wings when we know and passionately express our life's purpose.

Principles of Energy Management

Personal energy management is simple but not always easy. It consists of two phases: revitalization and deficiency avoidance.

The first step in Personal Energy Management is to identify situations that generate plenty of energy; things that recharge your batteries. The second step is to identify your "black holes", things that drain you dry.

Things that drive and motivate you, and things that drain and drag you down are what need to be identified in order to effect change. **D**rive and **D**rain are the 2 **D**'s of Energy Management.

Energy leaks are preventable most of the time. You do not need to go through life exhausted, stressed out or depressed. Effective Personal Energy Management stops energy waste and saves energy for people and activities that you really enjoy.

Step 1: Identify what Gives you Energy

Do you have memories of times when you felt passionately involved in a personal mission and confident that all was possible? Do you remember how alive and energetic you felt? If you do, you know what optimized personal energy feels like. There is nothing like passionate involvement to give you wings.

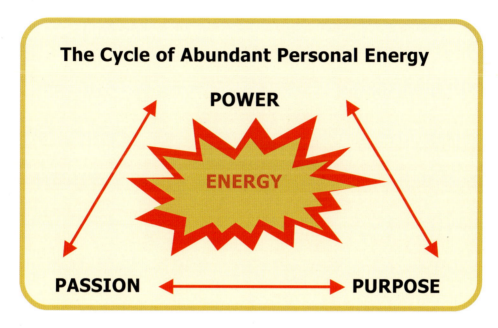

Fig 2: The *Cycle of Abundant Personal Energy*

Examples of situations when we feel energized:
☺ When we listen to our body and take care of its needs;
☺ When we feel supported and loved;
☺ When we are proud of ourselves;
☺ When we are confident about trusting others;
☺ When we believe in our capacity to manifest our dreams;
☺ When we know our source of power is limited only by our beliefs;
☺ When we know that anything is possible;
☺ ***When we love ourselves more than anyone else.***

Table 1: *Ways to increase your energy.*

Step 2: Identify the Black Holes that Drain Energy

Being deprived of energy when we are exhausted and empty makes us feel victimized, powerless, hopeless, resentful and cynical. Circumstances that drain us of all energy and take us to those all-time lows from which it takes days to recover are energy "black holes".

Here are some examples of "black holes" which sap personal energy:
- Abusive situations where we get hurt physically or emotionally;
- Confrontations with an authority figure who treats us like a child;
- Exhaustive angry outbursts;
- Loss of a job seen as caused by inadequacy;
- Relationship endings;
- Chronic senseless "tug of wars" for power.

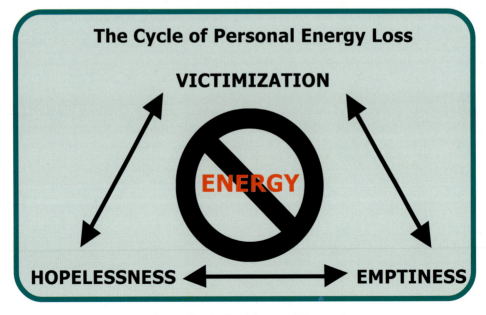

Fig. 3: The Cycle of Personal Energy Loss

> **Examples of circumstances that drain personal energy:**
>
> - ☹ hunger and tiredness
> - ☹ lack of regular exercise
> - ☹ lack of proper medical treatment
> - ☹ addiction
> - ☹ feeling victimized
> - ☹ feeling alone or abandoned
> - ☹ uselessly striving for unattainable goals
> - ☹ being inappropriately dependent on others
> - ☹ feeling cheated or taken advantage of
> - ☹ feeling trapped
> - ☹ feeling things won't change
> - ☹ being desperate or feeling hopeless
> - ☹ being cynical or bitter
> - ☹ feeling resentment
> - ☹ allowing obstacles to impede goal achievement
> - ☹ allowing past failure to interfere with the present
> - ☹ feeling too old, too young or too late
> - ☹ thinking you don't have what it takes
> - ☹ believing all is futile and thinking "What's the point?"
> - ☹ allowing being right to be more important than being happy
> - ☹ needing inappropriate approval from others
> - ☹ having no purpose and thinking, "There must be more to life"
> - ☹ believing you can't
> - ☹ not being able to say NO
> - ☹ experiencing life as difficult
> - ☹ working with unclear priorities
> - ☹ always compromising
> - ☹ settling for less
> - ☹ not daring to dream for fear of failure

Table 2: Ways to loose energy

Having Energy is experienced as:

- ☺ Vitality, Stamina, Vigor
- ☺ Power, Feeling Capable (I Can)
- ☺ Feeling connected, in the flow
- ☺ Feeling capable to take the lead
- ☺ Feeling attractive to others
- ☺ Self-Confidence
- ☺ Feeling supported
- ☺ Being creative
- ☺ Entrepreneurship
- ☺ Passion and drive
- ☺ Having purpose
- ☺ Being optimistic

Lack of Energy is experienced as:

- ☹ Tiredness, exhaustion
- ☹ Resignation, depression
- ☹ Aloofness, paralysis based on fear
- ☹ Feeling victimized and used
- ☹ Emptiness
- ☹ Being ridden with guilt or shame
- ☹ Isolation, loneliness
- ☹ Feeling abandoned, rejected
- ☹ Being cynical or full of despair
- ☹ Feeling resentful or acting hateful
- ☹ Feeling purposeless, hopelessness
- ☹ Feeling dead inside

Table 3: *Characteristics of people experiencing having or lacking energy*

The Personal Energy Crisis

Stop Personal Energy Leaks: Learn to Replenish

The most urgent thing to do when you first start bringing personal energy to your consciousness is to address your most important source of depletion, your most damaging black hole. If you have difficulty identifying that major leak yourself, get feedback from trusted friends or journal until it becomes clear. Journaling is a tool that will help you identify your energy-draining patterns on your own.

Most people have only 2 or 3 principle destructive patterns that affect their lives dramatically, but becoming aware of energy mismanagement is only the first step in a process of recovery and change. The second step is addressing what needs to be. Changing one's thinking patterns and behavior is particularly difficult, but this book presents you with tools that help.

Powerlessness is a debilitating emotional manifestation and the biggest obstacle that impedes change. In order to change a pattern, one has to believe they have the capacity to do just that. It is a power issue and involves ones confidence in ones own ability.

To be efficient at switching from a negative energy cycle to a positive one, it is necessary to have the courage to reclaim our own power and use it appropriately.

"If you believe you can, or if you believe you can't, you're absolutely right"

The Heart: Our Newest Frontier

> *"If you want to change, you've got to change."*
> G. Walker

Power has gained a bad reputation over the last century. There has been so much abuse and misuse of power that we have come to equate power with tyranny and dictatorship. Power in itself is neither good nor bad, it depends solely on the use one makes of it. Denying personal power because of previous abuse by those in power is like refusing to use electricity because one has been burned by an electrical appliance.

Powerless people have no choice but to see themselves as victims. They let others or circumstances have power over them and dictate their fate. Reclaiming personal power is an important step to becoming free to express ones potential.

Powerlessness is turned around by self-love and self-respect. Loving and respecting ourselves leads us to stop tolerating abuse and blaming others and to start tapping into the power of love to direct our lives. Self-love through heart energy is the key to increased personal power.

To summarize this chapter, personal energy management, which is emphasizing what is rejuvenating rather than giving in to people and circumstances that sap our energy, can only be achieved through self-love. In every challenging situation, the question we need to ask ourselves is *"What is the loving thing to do here?"* The answer to that question lies in our heart. In the next chapter, new discoveries on brain-heart communication will be shared, inviting you to use the loving power of your heart to successfully manage your energy.

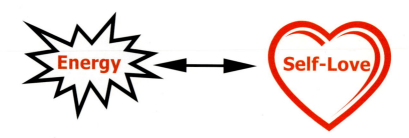

The Personal Energy Crisis

YOU ARE ENERGY: SHINE!

Chapter 2

Heart —Brain Synchronization

Latest Research on the Respective Roles of the Brain and the Heart

Energy-deficiency leaves us prey to stress-related illness. Modern life has devastating long-term effects on our bodies and souls, but we can tap into the tremendous underutilized healing capacities of our bodies in order to energize them and gain the advantage. This chapter takes a look at the latest discoveries in brain and heart physiology and how they impact our health and daily lives.

I- New Understandings of Human Brain Functioning

Latest discoveries in neuroscience have defined the roles of different areas of the brain and their interconnections. During the 90's, designated "the Brain Decade", new computer assisted imaging (CAT scan, PET scan and MRI) made brain mapping possible, which immensely increased our general understanding of the human brain. We now know which area of the brain is involved in specific tasks.

For example, Dr. David Servan-Schreiber[5], a neuropsychiatrist and pioneer in the field of cognitive neuroscience, helped locating the 'fear center' of the brain in the amygdala, a limbic structure of the central brain. These and other discoveries are examined here in the following overview of today's understanding of human brain function.

Human Brain

The nervous system includes the brain, the spinal cord and a network of nerves. The brain, weighing only about three pounds, is without a doubt the most complex organ of the body. Often depicted as the "conductor" orchestrating all vital functions of the body, it controls all voluntary activities (movements and speech), oversees unconscious and involuntary function (respiration, body temperature, digestion, immune system), supervises growth and tissue repair.

The Human Brain is Composed of Four Main Structures

1. The **Brainstem** regulates the autonomous nervous system, which operates without our conscious intervention. It is involved in controlling blood pressure and heart rate. As the **action** center of our brain, it integrates sensory-motor reflexes.

2. The **Central Brain,** including the **limbic structure,** is the **feeling** center; the fear center is located in the amygdala.

3. The **Neo-Cortex** is the **thinking** center and is also involved with speech.

4. The **Pre-frontal Lobes** integrate **higher intellectual function,** like abstract thinking, synthesis, analysis, and introspection.

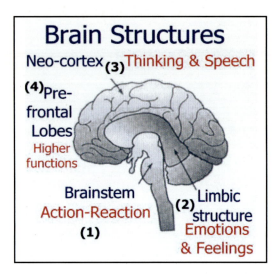

Figure 4: *The four structures of the human brain. The brainstem (1) is the action center and is in charge of survival. The limbic strutures of the central brain (2) are the feeling centers. The Neo-cortex (3) is the thinking center, also involved with speech. Finally, the pre-frontal lobes (4) are involved with higher intellectual functions.*

Evolution of the Human Brain

Mother Nature has a typical and unique way of building new structures; she builds on top of the old. When going from simple to complex, instead of starting a new design from scratch, she adds a new structure to the previous model. Human brain is thus composed of layers of structures, superimposed one on top of the other.

One of the oldest living organisms on the planet is the unicellular amoeba. Its rudimentary nervous system allows it to reach out to its environment for food. It can probe its surroundings and tell what is good and what is harmful. It also has the ability to react to avoid danger. This simple creature already has an information processing system in place, which enables it to gather information from both its internal and external environment. It makes decisions according to this information and takes action to incorporate or reject materials.

Heart –Brain Synchronization

Reptiles, moe evoleved, are creatures with more complex nervous system. They have a spinal cord and a tiny "reptilian brain", which operates in an action-reaction mode. When they detect danger, they react by instantly running away; the "fight or flight" reaction.

Primitive mammalians developed an emotional brain on top the reptilian brain, which was necessary for their survival. They needed to be capable of emotional bonding in order to protect their defenseless offspring. Emotions also fostered the development of primitive social structures, which made them more efficient at hunting and protecting their packs.

More evolved mammalians lik primates, added another layer to their brain, a neo-cortex wrapped around the central emotional brain. This top layer has become thicker and more convoluted in the human brain as the number of cells and the number of connections between them increased. With more brainpower, humans developed sophisticated tools and speech, giving them a definite competitive edge on the rest of the animal kingdom.

The last addition to the evolving brain structure was the pre-frontal lobes, whose exact role still eludes us. Its role seems to be involved with the integration and modulation of other parts of the brain. Some researchers postulate that the pre-frontal lobes are involved with affect regulation, the capacity to dissociate from one's emotion and to control reactions to those emotions. This mystery about the function of the pre-frontal lobes is at the core of the assertion that human beings only use 10% of their brain.

In summary, evolution has provided the human brain with many layers:

1. The **reptilian brain** composed of the spinal cord and the brainstem responsible for "fight or flight" reactions.

2. The **central brain** or limbic structures where emotions are spawned. These structures are in charge of unconscious physiologic processes, like blood pressure, heart rate, digestion, immunity and hormonal production, and are subject to emotional input.

3. The **neo-cortex** fostered articulate thinking, reasoning and speech.

4. The **pre-frontal lobes** of the cortex, whose roles are not clear but are possibly involved with affect regulation and capacity for transcendence.

Intellect and Emotions

As a result of Mother Nature's building process, modern man operates with a brain composed of multiple brain layers, inherited from all species that lived on the planet before him. It is not surprising that the integration of all these layers is a challenge. Impulses from our archaic brain are sometimes difficult to integrate with more evolved pre-frontal lobes superior functions; behaviors are not always congruent with higher intelligence. *"He is an intelligent person, why does he behave this way?"*

Human Impulse is Governed by 4 Distinct Legitimate Needs

1. Basic Survival needs, including the need to reproduce, are housed in our reptilian brain layer.

2. Emotional needs, like belonging and relating to others, initiates in the mammalian brain layer.

3. Intellectual needs, marked in human evolutionary development by the emergence of Homo Sapiens, allow us to develop speech, to take better control of our environment, and to communicate abstract thought.

4. The recently acquired **needs for actualization, freedom and service** are in the scope of modern research.

If we want to survive as a species, our biggest challenge at this time in our evolution is to be successful at integrating our emotions with our intellect. For centuries, these two functions have been in conflict, with reason overwhelmingly triumphing over emotion.

Since Descartes, the western world has left very little place for the expression of emotion, which is generally considered a sign of weakness and irrationality. The result of this aggressive intellectual override is a life void of meaning and joy, where health and family life are sacrificed to the gods of performance and accomplishment.

Stress is a consequence of the ongoing war between these two protagonists. The price we pay for poor stress management is extravagant in terms of dollars and lost opportunities for happiness.

Daniel Goleman[6], a pioneer in the field of Emotional Intelligence (EQ), is one of the first representatives of the scientific community to urge us to integrate cognition and emotions. According to Goleman, Emotional Intelligence can be measured by ones ability to identify emotions and understand their process, detach oneself from them, discuss them and manage them in a healthy way.

Emotional intelligence is based on the ability to know and understand emotions, and the ability to respond to emotions in a loving way. According to Goleman, emotional intelligence (EQ) is better indicator than IQ at predicting someone's ability to deal with everyday life challenges, level of satisfaction and sense of fulfillment.

Future Trends in Evolution of the Human Brain

The trend in brain evolution seems to be in the direction of integration; new connections between different areas that would allow for more complex and more sophisticated use of our brain. The little we know about pre-frontal lobes and their role in affect regulation is indicative of this trend. The future of human brain points in the direction of integrating many operational centers and synchronizing intellect with emotions.

Future Trends in Human Evolution:

1- the age of **Instinct** (Fear)

2- the age of **Reason** (Intellect)

3- future age of **Wisdom** (Heart-Brain Synchronization)

II- Heart Function: Recent Discoveries

In medical schools in the 60's, the heart was simply studied as a muscle that pumped blood through a complex system of arteries and veins. The role of the heart was to deliver oxygen and other nutrients to cells and to collect waste products and carry them to the liver and kidneys for elimination.

We were taught that blood pressure was produced by the fact that the heart is an intermittent pump. Blood circulation is caused by a difference in blood pressure, a gradient between full muscle contraction of the heart (systolic pressure) and the subsequent rest state of the heart muscle (diastolic pressure). At medical school, our cardiology classes were filled with notions of physics and biochemistry applied to the different roles of that pump.

Cardio-Endocrinology (Heart as an Endocrine Gland)

In the 70's, Drs Genest and Cantin[7] of the Montreal Research Institute discovered that the heart was also a hormone-producing endocrine gland. One of these hormones called ANF helps control blood pressure, influences the immune system and plays a role in maintaining balance between the sympathetic and parasympathetic nervous systems that we will describe later. They also discovered that the heart contains "ICA" cells that, like the brain, produce adrenaline and dopamine.

Recently, it was found the heart produces oxytocin (also called the "love hormone") in the same amount as the brain. This hormone plays an important role in mother-child bonding during breast-feeding and is also key to the socialization process of a child. Oxytocin seems to play an active role in bonding lovers, also.

Electromagnetic Fields

The heart generates a powerful electromagnetic field.

When I was a teenager, the following science project was part of the curriculum. A frog was put to sleep and a heart cell was isolated and observed under a microscope. This heart cell was beating on its own, even isolated from the rest of the heart. This isolated heart cell could continue beating for a few minutes, but eventually would stop in a spasmodic contraction (fibrillation).

If at that moment another freshly picked heart cell were put close (but not touching) to the fibrillating one, the latter would start beating at the same pace. This can only be explained by the effect of the electromagnetic field of the beating cell on the dying one.

This pacing effect is called 'entrainment'. "Cardiac coherence", a phenomenon that we will discuss later, is based on the entrainment capacity of the heart.

Every living organism has an electromagnetic field but that of the heart is exceptionally powerful. The heart is composed of millions of small synchronous generators producing a 2.5-watt current with each heartbeat, enough to light a small light bulb.

The amplitude of the current produced by the heart is 50 times larger than that of the brain. This becomes evident when an ECG (electro-cardiogram, measuring the electric activity of the heart) is compared with an EEG (electroencephalogram, measuring that of the brain). The electromagnetic field of the heart can be detected up to 15 feet outside of the body.

A mother holding a child in her arms keeps him within her electromagnetic field and vice versa. Lovers embracing each other do the same. A fetus is constantly bathed in the heart field of its mother and the energetic exchanges that are taking place during pregnancy are indelible.

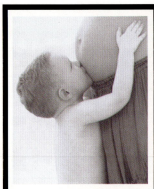

Embryology of the Heart and the Brain

My research on the new roles of the heart and the brain led me to study their respective development in the uterus and to understand the chronological formation of these two organs.

In human embryos, both the heart and the brain start forming at the beginning of the third week of gestation, but they stem from different types of cells. The first heartbeats are observed around the 22nd day.

The heart is the first organ of the body to function.

At this time, the first nerve cells are forming in the primitive neural tube and there is no connection between the embryonic nervous system and the beating heart. They form simultaneously but in different areas of the embryo. It is definitely not the embryonic brain that orders the heart to start beating. The heart's ability to contract is autonomous and heartbeats are self-generated. Because there are no nerves or blood vessels to connect those two organs at that early stage, the only means of communication is through their respective electromagnetic communication.

Neurocardiology (Science of the Heart's Brain)

More recently, researchers have paid closer attention to the connections and communications between the heart and other organs, including the brain.

Neurocardiology was born from studies of the heart's nervous system. Dr Armour[8] of Montreal University has published extensively on this new topic. It is now generally acknowledged that the heart is more than a pump that delivers oxygenated blood to the tissues.

This complex organ is a self-managed data processing center. It acts like a "little brain". With each heartbeat, it registers and sends information to the brain and other organs.

The exchange of information between the "heartbrain" and the rest of the body is done in three ways: via a **network of nerves (**the afferent branches of the autonomous nervous system); via **hormonal secretion** and via an **electromagnetic field** the heart itself generates.

The heart's nervous system components are the **intrinsic and** extrinsic systems. The **intrinsic system** is a network of nervous tissue, nodes and nerves that transmit electrical current through the heart muscle.

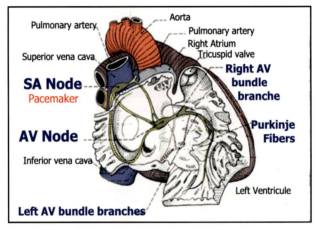

Figure 5: The heart's intrinsic nervous system. The Pacemaker emits an electrical signal that is carried in the cardiac muscle through the bundle branches and the Purkinje fibers; the result is synchronized contraction of the muscle that thrusts the blood out.

This network includes:
- the **SA (Sinuatrial) node** or pacemaker, located in the right atrium;
- the **AV (Atrioventricular) node**, located at the junction between the right atria and the ventricular;
- the **AV (Atrioventricular) bundle** branches, conduction nerves inside both ventricles and
- the **Purkinje Fibers**, conduction nerves deep inside the heart muscle.

The natural pacemaker of the heart, or SA node, sends an electrical signal that will trigger contractions of the heart muscle, thus generating heartbeats at a frequency of 70-80 per minute.

The electrical impulse is then transmitted to the AV node and further down to the heart muscle through the deep ramifications of the bundle branches and the Purkinje fibers. This propagation of electrical flux produces contraction of the muscle in sequence, which generates blood circulation throughout the body.

This nervous complex allows the heart to function like a 'brain outside the brain' and to operate as an independent information processor: **the heart feels, learns and has memory**. This ability to process information, to experience emotions and to communicate is referred to as "**intelligence of the heart**".

On the other hand, the heart's **extrinsic nervous system** or autonomous nervous system (ANS) consists of two sections: the **sympathetic** and **parasympathetic** systems distributed along the spine and at the base of the skull.

When the sympathetic system is activated, we are alert and ready to "fight or flight". If, on the other hand, the parasympathetic system is activated, we are in recuperation and restoration mode, relaxed like a cat cuddled in front of the fireplace.

Parasympathetic system at work: there is nothing like a "catnap" after a good meal...

Heart rhythm constantly reflects the inter-dynamics of these two systems. The parasympathetic slows heartbeat, while the sympathetic system accelerates it. The ANS (autonomous nervous system) interacts not only with the heart and blood vessels, but also with the digestive, hormonal and immune systems. Our thoughts and emotions can threaten its delicate balance at any moment.

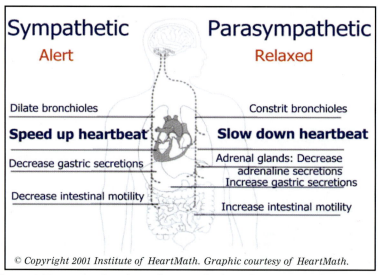

Figure 6: Respective functions of sympathetic and parasympathetic systems.

The Brain Can Influence the Heart

It has been long established that brain activity can influence the heart. A fearful thought, or a nightmare, makes the heart go faster. A number of health issues are caused by sympathetic/parasympathetic imbalances including stress related disorders. Emotions, positive or negative, influence this balance. Anger, for example, activates the sympathetic system and turns off the parasympathetic system, resulting in a constriction of the arteries. An angry person is at risk of high blood pressure and heart attacks if anger becomes habitual and chronic.

The Heart Can Influence the Brain

Since the 60's researchers documented the reverse: *the heart can influence the brain*. A network of afferent nerves that connect the heart to the brain has been identified. It is a complex intrinsic nervous system consisting of several types of nerve cells, including cells capable of producing neurotransmitters. *The heart has the ability to either accelerate or slow down brain activity.*

This intrinsic nervous system translates heart data (heartbeat, blood pressure, etc.) into electrical, chemical, electromagnetic and hormonal signals and data, which are then forwarded to the brain via afferent pathways.

The Heart Communicates with the Brain

Constant bidirectional communication between the heart and the brain influences brain activity and organ function. The heart and its 'little brain' communicates with and influences the brain and other organs. Heart-brain communication leads to better integration of their respective intelligences:

1. the *intelligence of the brain* in the form of intellect, c o g n i t i o n and its emotions: fear, anger, shame, guilt and anxiety

2. the *intelligence of the heart* in the form of wisdom, knowing, intuition, compassion, gratitude, love, joy and peace.

The heart is a sophisticated data processing center that plays a pivotal role in connecting the intellect, the emotions and the body. Leading-edge research is presently studying the integration of body, brain and heart.

The heart has the electrical and chemical means to reach and affect our perception and the power to shape our experience, thereby impacting everyday human life.

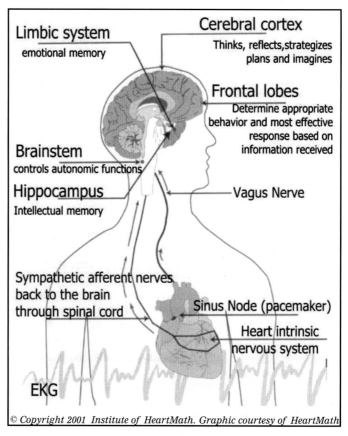

Figure 7: Heart to brain communication system. The human body has numerous sensory systems, which send information back to the brain. The heart communicates to the brain in two ways: through the vagus nerve and through the afferent branches of the sympathetic system.

Heart –Brain Synchronization

Scientifically studied techniques have been developed to help to reach heart-brain-body integration. These techniques foster harmony between the activity of the brain and the heart. This state of harmonious integration has been called *"cardiac coherence"* and will be further discussed in Chapter 3.

Cardiac coherence helps improve bidirectional communication between the heart and the brain. It also balances the sympathetic and parasympathetic systems, which regulate heartbeat and blood pressure.

In the state of cardiac coherence, the heart has an energizing effect on the brain. The brain is more effective at integrating new information, retrieving stored information and becoming more efficient at problem solving and decision-making.

Cardiac coherence is an exceptional stress management tool, which greatly improves intellectual capacity, clears thinking, focuses concentration, betters problem solving abilities, augments creativity and increases productivity. Lets have a closer look at it.

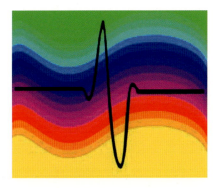

Chapter 3

Cardiac Coherence

Coherence describes a state of congruence between different functions. Cardiac coherence refers to an alignment and synchronization between the heart, the brain and all the other organs that interact with them. The result of sustained cardiac coherence is better functioning of all organs, improved physiology and psychological balance.

To achieve a state of cardiac coherence, one must harmonize the brain with the heart and enhance their respective functions. As seen in the previous chapter, the heart has the ability to influence brain activity and hormonal production. Cardiac coherence uses the powerful energy of the heart to induce changes in the brain. It is therefore a powerful tool for personal energy enhancement.

People who learn to achieve a state of cardiac coherence can expect to:
❖ Engage their hearts to manage stressful situations and avoid stress related illnesses;
❖ Improve their emotional health and the quality of their relationships;
❖ Be generally in a good mood and emotionally stable;
❖ Think clearly, focus and make decisions effortlessly;
❖ Improve creativity, productivity and efficiency;
❖ Improve memory and learning capacity;
❖ Improve problem solving abilities and
❖ Play an active role in decreasing violence in their community.

Physiological Basis of Cardiac Coherence

Heart rhythms are not perfectly regular. Heart rates (like 80 per min.) represent only an average of the beat-to-beat changes. Cardiac coherence is measured by studying variations in heart rhythms. When those variations are irregular, they are said to be chaotic. Cardiac coherence is obtained when the variations have a harmonious rhythm.

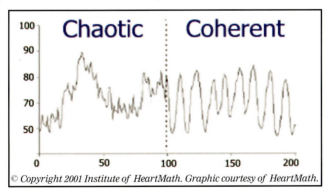

Figure 8: *Chaotic heart rhythm pattrens on the left and coherent rhythms on the right.*

The studies done on heart rhythm variations show a definite connection to emotional states[9]. Stressful emotions like fear, anger or guilt affect heart rhythm and produce negative effects on organ function and the immune system. On the other hand, cardiac coherence, based on "heart-felt" positive emotions, restores harmony among different body functions, which, in turn, enhances health.

The Heart: Our Newest Frontier

Techniques to Achieve Cardiac Coherence

The Institute HeartMath[10] of California has done extensive research on the effect of cardiac coherence on human physiology. Researchers have developed techniques that induce cardiac coherence and have applied them to stress management, health, mental health, education and violence prevention in the family and community.

Cardiac coherence-inducing techniques are based on the scientifically proven concept that the heart has the ability to schift the brain toward optimum functioning.

Studies[11] have shown an entrainment effect of the heart on brain activity. Comparing the ECG and EEG of subjects practicing coherence-inducing techniques, they demonstrated that the EEG (representing brain activity) of those subjects was changing and synchronizing with heart rhythm.

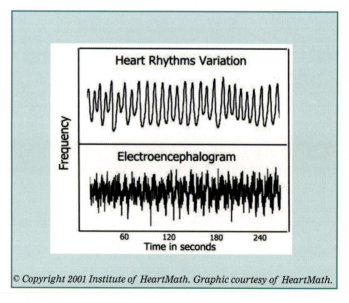

Figure 9: Heart rhythms and brain activity can become synchronized, as demonstrated here by EEG, harmonyzing with heart rhythm variations.

Cardiac Coherence

The practice of these cardiac coherence-inducing techniques involves the higher emotions of the heart, like appreciation, empathy and compassion, which help balance the autonomous nervous system[12]. As individuals learn to sustain sincere "heart-focused" states of appreciation or empathy, the brain's electrical activity can be paced by the entrainment effect of the heart rhythms.

The experience of these emotions produces cardiac coherence, which in turn harmonizes the autonomous nervous system and thus improves the function of all organs involved, including immune and hormonal systems.

As previously stated, emotions, either positive or negative, can influence the variations of heart rhythms. The higher emotions experienced during the practice of coherence-inducing techniques have the power to synchronize the heart-brain system, improve the brain's ability to process information and enhance cognitive function, thereby, facilitating learning. Balanced brain chemistry optimizes the functioning of all systems involved, thus improving health[13].

The Heart: Our Newest Frontier

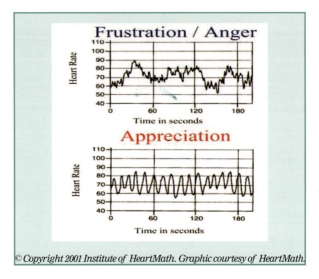

Figure 10: *Frustration and anger produce irregular heart rhythms. Appreciation creates harmonious and coherent heat rhythms on the frequency chart.*

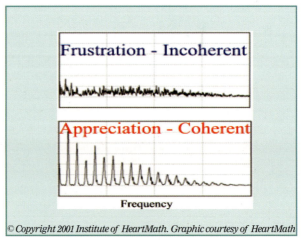

Figure 11: *The top graph is a typical spectrum analysis of the electrocardiogram (ECG) showing the frequencies generated by the heart when a person experiences **frustration**. This is called an incoherent spectrum because the frequencies are scattered and distorted. The bottom graph shows the frequency analysis of the ECG during a period when a person is experiencing deep, sincere **appreciation**. This is called a coherent spectrum because the power is ordered and harmonious.*

Training Biofeedback Software

Biofeedback software called "Freeze Framer"[14] has been developed by the Institute of HeartMath. The Freeze Framer helps users master cardiac coherence techniques. A fingertip sensor reads heart rate information and feeds it to the software. Real-time feedback is given, which allows quick monitoring of the learning process.

Cardiac coherence is studied by using heart rate variation (HRV) as an indicator of heart dynamics. Analysis of HRV gives a direct non-invasive method of observing heart-brain interaction and achievable coherence states.

The graphs generated give a visual representation of the degree of coherence attained during the practice of the technique; it also allows monitoring and comparing the progress of consecutive sessions[15]. This software is very useful for applied research purposes and has been successfully used to demonstrate the effects of coherence-inducing techniques in the areas of health and stress management in schools and in the workplace.

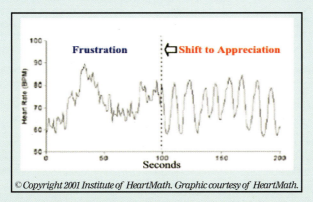

Figure 12: *Emotions are reflected in heart rhythm patterns. Note the shift from an erratic heart rhythm pattern associated with frustration to a smooth, harmonious, sine wave-like (coherent) pattern as the individual uses the positive "emotion-refocusing" technique and purposely generates a heartfelt feeling of appreciation.*

Coherence is Contagious

Researchers at the Institute of HeartMath also demonstrated the influence of the heart's electric activity on two people at conversational distance. A person who has achieved cardiac coherence can influence the electric activity of the brain and the heart of another person[16].

The next two graphics show the electrical heart activity (ECG) of subject-1 influencing the brain activity (EEG) of subject-2.

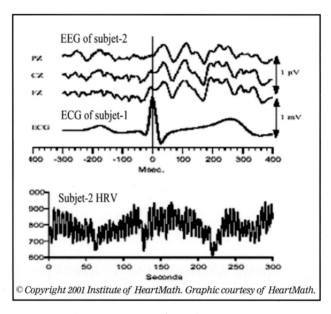

Figure 13: This set of graphs shows an example of the heart-brain synchronization that can occur between two people at conversational distance. The top three traces are subject-2's brainwaves, which are synchronized to subject-1 ECG (heartbeat signal). The lower graph is a sample of subject-2's heart rhythm pattern, which was coherent throughout the majority of the record.

Cardiac Coherence

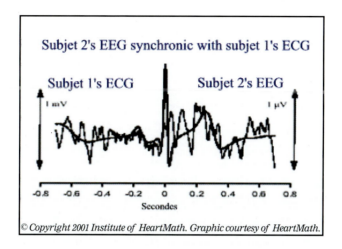

Figure 14: *This graphic is an overlay plot of the same EEG and ECG data shown in Figure 11. Note the similarity of the wave shapes, indicating a high degree of synchronization.*

Family members often experience heart synchronization.

Cardiac Coherence Induces Changes in Perception

"Change your perception and change your experience"
Deepak Chopra, MD

Many studies have established that the quantity of stress experienced in any given situation depends on the emotional reaction to the situation, much more than on the situation itself. Stress levels are directly related to amounts of negative emotion experienced.

After an earthquake, for example, victims do not all react the same way. Their reactions are not consistent with the amount of loss they suffered, but are proportionate to the level of emotional turmoil they endured. The long-term consequences of a disaster are in direct correlation with the level of emotional pain victims report having experienced, the level of stress they endured. Their perception of the event is responsible for the level stress they experienced.

By addressing perception, we can influence stress levels. Cardiac coherence helps change perception[17] by focusing on positive emotions. Broader and compassionate perception is key to reducing the risk of post-traumatic stress-related illness.

*House chore or fun activity?
It's all a matter of perception.*

Practicing coherence-inducing techniques brings about change in the way people perceive and manage difficult situations. For those who practice these techniques, the world stops being antagonistic and life ceases to be a battle.

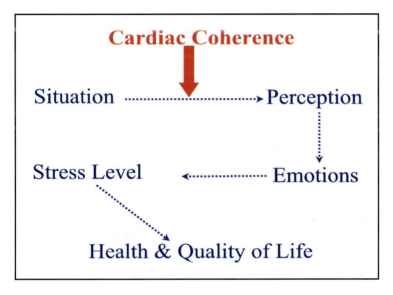

Figure 15: *Cardiac coherence produces a shift in perception, which creates an impact on the stress level perceived and, thus, on the quality of one's experience of life.*

*Life is to be enjoyed.
Quality matters.*

Clinical Research and Applications of Cardiac Coherence-Inducing Techniques

The Freeze-Framer software allowed the Institute of HeartMath's program trainers to visually demonstrate the effectiveness of their heart-coherence techniques. Impressive case studies have been conducted by HeartMath using their technique in a variety of professional areas such as health care, education and business, where significant benefits have been documented.

Each study had a different goal depending on the area of intervention. When working with health professionals, HeartMath's trainers aimed at reducing stress, anxiety or depression, chronic fatigue and blood pressure. When working with schools, they sought to improve academic grades, self-confidence and to reduce violent behavior. When working with managers and business leaders, the goal was to increase productivity and creativity at work.

A. Health-Related Clinical Research

Current research reveals an increase in the prevalence of diseases caused by autonomic nervous system dysfunction. Many of these, like hypertension, coronary disease, cardiac arrhythmia, sudden cardiac death, sleep disorders, diabetes, and others, are worsened by stress and negative emotion.

On the other hand, positive emotion and effective emotional management skills have been shown to prolong health and significantly reduce premature mortality[18, 19].

Moreover, a growing number of studies show that patients who are exposed to cardiac coherence techniques, even for a short time, improve clinically and symptomatically[20, 21].

B. Cardiac Coherence-Inducing Techniques in Business

Cardiac coherence training sessions have been implemented in a wide range of practical settings in the workplace. High tech companies, government agencies, hospitals, banks and multinationals have introduced these techniques to their personnel as part of an "Inner Quality Management" program, where individuals learn to maintain a coherent internal environment.

Motorola[22], Cal PERS (Government agency)[23], Santa Clara County Police Officers[24], Royal Dutch Shell and the Canadian Imperial Bank of Commerce (CIBC) are some of the companies who have implemented this program.

The Heart: Our Newest Frontier

Thousands of managers and employees have been trained in cardiac coherence-inducing techniques and have reported benefits to health and quality of life issues at work and at home.

By learning to synchronize their hearts and brains, these workers have been able to control their internal environment through the synergy of intellectual, intuitive and emotional intelligence. The result has been increased productivity and more pleasant work environments.

These are some of the benefits reported:

❖ Improved work performance,
❖ Increased vitality,
❖ Greater confidence, balance and clarity under stress,
❖ Improved communication,
❖ Greater cooperation within work teams,
❖ Reduced distress and fatigue,
❖ Reduced sleeplessness and physical stress symptoms,
❖ Improved listening and relationships with family.

Employees who learn to engage their heart experience greater cooperation within work teams.

C. Cardiac Coherence-Inducing Techniques in Education

Our educational systems focus on improving children's cognitive skills from the moment they enter the kindergarten classroom. But virtually no emphasis is placed on educating children in the management of the inner conflict and unbalanced emotions they experience each school day.

As new concepts such as emotional intelligence become more widely applied and understood, more educators are realizing that cognitive ability is not the sole or necessarily the most critical determinant of success in today's society.

Middle school students in Florida[25] and High school seniors in Minnesota[26] were trained in cardiac coherence-inducing techniques. As a result, they improved their intellectual and emotional management skills.

These studies demonstrate that when physiological coherence is increased through heart-brain synchronization, mental and emotional turmoil are better managed by the students, thereby, fostering greater mental clarity and expanding the mental capacity.

The Heart: Our Newest Frontier

Besides improving grades, these young people improved skills in three main areas:

1. Personal attitudes: Students developed better attitude while at school, more self-confidence, self-reliance, self-satisfaction and assertiveness, better emotional control and became better at managing stressful situations.

2. Interpersonal skills: Students became more outgoing and empathetic, nicer to classmates and better at anger management. Peer support increased and students participated more and obeyed better.

3. Achievement aptitude: Students became better motivated and more energetic, better focused, better at managing their work and developed better leadership skills.

These results and changes in attitudes were observed at school and also at home[27]. With more easily manageable students, teachers' comfort levels also improved. Schools, homes and the community as a whole, all benefited from the practice of these techniques.

These research studies show that learning cardiac coherence-inducing techniques can help in many areas. Once mastered, they can reduce stress, improve health, enhance mental capacity, at work and at school, improve the quality of relationships and enhance the quality of life in general at home and in the community.

Section 2

Heart-Smiling

Chapter 4

Heart-Smiling

Heart-Smiling is a simple technique that fosters the state of cardiac coherence. The intelligence of the brain and the intelligence of the heart work together to synchronize and harmonize function. Derived from the cardiac-inducing techniques taught by the Institute of HeartMath, Heart-Smiling adds a smiling element that reinforces its capacity to improve health, reduce stress, enhance relationships and radically transform personal experience.

Heart-Smiling triggers an inside smile that very often also appears on the lips and in ones eyes. This "inside smile" is a tribute to the "Presence", an inner intelligence and loving energy at the core of our being. To be "present in Presence" is the essence of any meditation, whose goal is to transform inner emotional climate and access a peaceful, joyful transcendental state. Contact with this "Presence" opens the floodgates of a powerful revitalizing energy.

Heart-Smiling enables its practitioners to experience love, compassion, gratitude, joy and peace. Through the experience of these higher emotions, people channel the powerful energy of the heart and transform perception and attitude.

"Don't wait to be happy to smile. Smile, then you'll be happy"
Edward L. Kramer

THE 3 STEPS OF HEART-SMILING

1. Bring your attention to your heart and breathe effortlessly from the center of your chest. Become aware of your thoughts, feelings and sensations. Identify any discomfort.

2. Focus again on breathing from the heart. Bring to your memory a person or a situation that made your heart "sing". It could be a moment of intense joy, gratitude, profound peace, touching love or compassion. Experience those higher emotions again, right now, and surrender to the warm pleasant feeling this exercise generates.
Let a smile emerge to your lips.

3. Pay attention to the physical changes taking place in your body. Note any change in attitude and perception. If you are dealing with a challenging situation, take advantage of this heart connection to **ask Heart to guide you to the appropriate solution.**

Table 4: *The 3 steps of Heart-Smiling*

Heart-Smiling

Heart-Smiling's 3 Easy Steps:

1. Bring Your Attention to the Heart Area in the middle of your chest and take two deep relaxing breaths. Then breathe normally and effortlessly. Feel your breath going naturally into and out of your heart. If you are facing another person, imagine your breath circulating smoothly in a figure 8 shape between your two hearts.

The *physical heart* (where one feels palpitations) is also the space of the *emotional heart* (where one feels elated, broken hearted, etc.) and the space of the *spiritual heart* (where one is touched, moved, etc.). Heart energy (physical, emotional and spiritual) are all present in adjacent areas in the middle of your chest.

Breathing from your heart helps you become more centered and in the present moment.

Monitor your feelings and sensations; identify any discomfort. Become aware of your thoughts and emotions. It is useful to ask a few questions in order to better understand the situation: *"What's going on?"* or *"What am I afraid of?"* Asking questions is a process that removes you from the emotional turmoil by bringing you "into your head". Use your intellect to gather and analyze information about the content of your thoughts and feelings.

This questioning process allows you to become an observer of a stressful situation you are engaged in and to suspend your emotional involvement. As an observer, it is easier to have a broader pereption of the present situations unfolding on the stage of your life. You can become aware that you are more than the main actor, you are also the director and producer of the play presently unfolding: you can change the script at any moment. Becoming your "observer-self" allows you to stay uninvolved emotionally from the scene, to stop being engulfed by the drama and to refrain from being judgmental.

2. Come Back to Your Breathing from the Heart. Bring a person or situation from memory that "**made your heart sing**", a circumstance where you experienced **love, joy, peace, gratitude or compassion.** Make a genuine effort to experience these emotions again, right now when you need them. These higher emotions of the heart will raise you above the situation, above fear and resentment. They will help you be free of the need to be right or to prove your point.

When your heart is overflowing with higher emotion energy, your heart rhythm becomes harmonious and the communication with your brain and other organs is facilitated. This is the moment of cardiac coherence. Your whole body is then flooded with 'feel-good' hormones, like endorphins, that foster feelings of peace and empathy.

At that point, **let a smile emerge to your lips**. Only the heart with its superior emotions can trigger this type of smile: a touching smile of respect and compassion. This smile is irresistible and disarming!

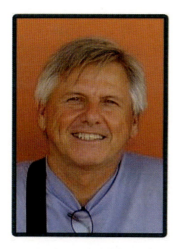

An irresistable and touching smile can disarm.

Warm heartedness is the key to happiness.
Dalaï Lama

Heart-Smiling

3. Pay attention to the changes taking place in your body, your attitude and your perception of the situation. Take the time to make mental note of the effect your smile has on your perception of the situation. Observe your posture and the non-verbal signals you are sending out. Take note also of your "mindscape", your internal mental and emotional state.

If the situation at hand needs resolution, **ask your Heart to guide you to the appropriate solution**. Decision-making is made easy when done in a state of heart-brain coherence. Decisions taken with your heart feel right. They are in alignment with your higher intelligence, intuition, values and aspirations.

Heart-Smiling is an introspective and reflective activity, which opens doors to the non-physical, spiritual dimension of self. Because it allows one to be present in Presence, it is a meditative activity and brings those who practice all the same beneficial effects.

What differentiates Heart-Smiling from standard meditation is that it is done with ones eyes open in the middle of a situation. It is not necessary to withdraw into a quiet place. Eyes, mind and heart are open to other people and the outside world. Heart-Smiling is an "open" meditation.

The language of the heart is silence, a smiling benevolent silence.

Heart-Smiling connects us to the internal Universal Life Force in our hearts and the hearts of others. Practicing Heart-Smiling becomes a "Namasté" salutation. Namasté is a Hindu spiritual salutation. It means: "The Divine Light in me recognizes and honors the Divine Light in you and in all beings". Heart-Smiling connects us to our own heart energy and to that same energy in others.

Practicing Heart-Smiling helps raise consciousness of our communities. The luminous eyes and bright smiles of people who consciously use the Heart-Smiling technique contagiously connect them to everyone in their environment and stimulate change. As they touch others, these new hearts enter into harmony, adopt the new warm positive rhythm and begin harmonizing the hearts of everyone with whom they come in contact. The effects of Heart-Smiling, thereby, spread exponentially throughout the community.

"A smile is less expensive than electricity, but it brings as much light"
L'Abbé Pierre

Characteristics of a Smile Emanating from the Heart

Heart-Smiling triggers a smile that may externalize on your lips. Such a smile will have the characteristic described in Table 5, which are associated with the higher emotions of the heart.

A Smile from the Heart is:
☺ respectful
☺ humble
☺ generous
☺ free
☺ contagious
☺ disarming
☺ reassuring
☺ peaceful
☺ touching
☺ compassionate
☺ tender
☺ powerful and efficient

A Smile from the Heart is not:
☹ supplicating
☹ insisting
☹ controlling
☹ flirtatious
☹ mischievous
☹ forced
☹ ironic
☹ sarcastic
☹ superior
☹ manipulative
☹ seductive
☹ faked

Table 5: *Characteristics of a Smile coming from the Heart*

Love Has the Power to Displace Fear

It is impossible for the heart to maintain two contradictory emotions at the same time. If gratitude is the prevailing emotion, there is no room for resentment, fear, self-doubt or anger. In order for fear to vanish from the heart, we need to replace it with love. A "Conscious Smile" from the Heart replaces fear-based emotion with love.

If the heart cannot simultaneously contain two contradicting emotions, love and fear cannot be present at the same time. By inducing a state of cardiac coherence through Heart-Smiling, higher emotions push fear away. Love melts fear, like the warm spring sun melts the snow, or like darkness disappears when light comes into a room.

If love or gratitude fills your heart, you will see others with love-tinted glasses. In life, we "reap what we sow". When love and gratitude fill our hearts, we attract love and gratitude. If a loving relationship is what we are looking for, we must fill our hearts first with love and generosity.

An Antidote to Fear

'Thank You' are two magic words. The magic wand of gratitude transforms experience and is the antidote to pain. When you feel gratitude in your heart, fear and insecurity melt way. Harboring a grateful heart is the means to end suffering. Pain is part of life. Suffering, the emotional aggravation of pain, is optional. A grateful heart is the key to enjoying a peaceful life.

"A smile is a secret key that opens many hearts"
Baden-Powell

Heart-Smiling

Heart-Smiling Training

Though very simple, the practice of "Heart-Smiling" does not always come easy. Like any technique, a training process is mandatory. The training process consist of four levels of practice:

> ❖ Level 1: alone in a calm situation.
>
> ❖ Level 2: alone in a difficult situation.
>
> ❖ Level 3: in the presence of another person, in a calm situation.
>
> ❖ Level 4: in the presence of another person, in conflicting situation.

Table 6: *Levels of practice of Heart-Smiling*

First, practice when you are alone, and then practice while interacting with others. Start with easy non-conflicting situations and gradually progress towards situations that are emotionally more challenging.

It is important to practice on a regular basis and as many times a day as possible until you master the technique. At some point, you will notice that you have begun to operate from the heart most of the time, and that a smile comes spontaneously to your lips, even in a crisis situation.

The benefits of practicing Heart-Smiling are instantaneous and immeasurable. As life is transformed by self-confidence and optimism, others lose their power to manipulate and control us. We look at others differently and see them with eyes of empathy and compassion. *A touched heart is a transformed heart.*

Warning! Possible Negative Reactions to Your Smile

Smiles can be misinterpreted depending on the context and past programming of the receivers. Distrustful people can be offended by a smile. *"What are you laughing at?"* can be the surprising response to heartfelt expression. People sometimes think we are making fun of them or that we are being condescending. We might be taken aback if we have not learned to anticipate those possible negative reactions. People with low self-esteem easily feel threatened by a smile and become defensive as they perceive smiles as judgmental.

How to React to a Defensive Person

Empathy (the ability to understand the fear and defense mechanisms of others) is needed to avoid confrontation. Becoming humble and non-threatening (*"I'm sorry, I didn't mean to offend you…."*) and showing compassion will help reduce tension and change the perception of defensive people.

How to React to a Person Unskilled at Reading Signals

Smiling is a very powerful lure. Abusive persons, unskilled at respecting boundaries, may read our smiles as invitations to intimacy: *"She smiles at me, therefore, she wants me"*. Unfortunately, these people have a very hard time taking "No" for an answer. In these cases, the appropriate reaction is to stop smiling and send very clear signals that intimacy is not what you are trying to achieve. Setting clear limits is an important skill when dealing with confused people. Self-defense courses teach us that, when dealing with confused people, firmness in setting very clear limits is the strategy of choice.

Heart-Smiling

A smile never goes unnoticed. When appreciated, a smile is usually rewarded with another smile. But, when a smile is misinterpreted, it can be refused. As the smile giver, you have to be prepared for both possibilities and not let refusal dishearten you. It is always sad to see one of your gifts being refused; but it is important to respect other people's capacity to receive.

Keep in mind that those who cannot accept your smile are precisely those who need it most. Be patient, save your smiles for times when these people are more open and ready to receive them.

A smile never goes unnoticed.

❋ ❋ ❋ ❋ ❋ ❋ ❋

The next chapter includes more information on the anatomy, the physiology, the development and roles of a smile. Though this information is not mandatory to the successful practice of Heart-Smiling, some may find it a useful tool in grasping the significance, value and impact of smiling consciously from the heart.

Heart-Smiling

Chapter 5

Physiology and Function of a Smile

Who is not totally charmed by the smile of a child? The innocence of that smile is what makes it so extremely powerful. Innocence melts away all barriers we put up to protect our hearts. Resistance is futile!

Figure 16: *Smile and the whole world smiles with you...*

A smile is an important physiognomic feature of non-verbal communication. Smiles are both universal and effective at sending messages of welcome and peace.

Physiology and Function of a Smile

> *"Man does not have a more definite mark of his nobility than a certain refined, silent smile, revealing of highest philosophy."*
> — Ernest Renan

It is a challenge to give definition to this universal phenomenon of smiling and to describe it in simple terms. The Merriam Webster Dictionary gives the following definitions of smile:

1: *a facial expression in which the eyes brighten and the corners of the mouth curve slightly upward expressing amusement, pleasure, approval and (sometimes) scorn;*

2 : *a pleasant or encouraging facial expression.*

All literary attempts to define smiling refer to many of the higher emotions we discussed earlier like joy, satisfaction, happiness, affection, amusement and pleasure. This facial expression is linked to a vast plethora of emotions.

Smiles play an active role in bonding and socialization. While the scientific community largely ignores smiling because of the lack of pharmaceutical application and profitability, psychology testing uses this important non-verbal expression as a marker for well-being.

> *"A smile is the universal language of goodness"*
> — William Arthur Ward

Developmental Stages

Child-psychologists Jean Piaget, John Bowlby and Rene Spitz have helped us understand the stages of development and evolution of smiling. During the first months of life, smiling develops in four different stages:
1. Spontaneous reflex smiling
2. Non-selective social smiling
3. Selective social smiling
4. Differential smiling

Figure 17: Newborn's "smiling at angels"

1. Spontaneous reflex smiling appears during the first hours after birth. Smiling is a newborn reflex like sucking and grasping. At this stage, smiling is not directed at anyone, babies seem to be 'smiling at angels'.

Physiology and Function of a Smile

The brain of newborns is not yet wired for peripheral vision; they can only focus on shapes about 10 to 15 inches from their eyes. Mother Nature has selected a focal range that is the distance between the face of the mother and that of her baby when she holds it in her arms, putting baby within the electromagnetic field of her heart.

2. Non-selective social smiling becomes more and more complex during baby's first few months according to Bowlby[28]. Prattle, glances and arm and leg movement complement this facial expression. During this period, mothers interact at a new level with their babies. Bonding takes place and the adult response to a child's smile builds the basis for future socializing. When a child is blind at birth, the reflex smile of the newborn tends to slowly fade away with time, suggesting that reflex smiling needs to be persistently stimulated by imitation and response from interacting adults. If blindness happens later, the child will keep his smiling abilities acquired at this early phase.

Figure 18: Non-selective smile during the first months of life.

Heart-Smiling

3. Selective social smiling starts at the age of six months, when a child is able to identify a specific face, usually the mother's or father's face.

At that point, it will stop smiling back at strangers.

For Piaget[29] this stage of baby smiling at familiar faces is a kind of 'déjà vu' reaction. Spitz[30], however, believes the recognition of specific facials traits is what triggers smiling.

Figure 19: Selective smile to parents.

At six months, a child's development enables it to make the link between its smile and the emotional reactions it triggers; its first experiment in human communication. A unique communication style is established with caretakers.

4. Differential smiling appears around the ninth month and will last a lifetime. This kind of smile occurs during interactions with familiar faces. It is adapted to situations and responds to positive reinforcement. Complexity and subtlety are developed during those interactions. Smiling is learned by imitation and interaction. Later in life, the ability to smile depends on the quality of the smile received during the first months of life.

Figure 20: Differential smiles that last a lifetime.

Anatomy of a Smile

Many facial muscles are involved when smiling. According to Rouvière, a French anatomist, emotion is translated into muscular movements of the face (expression). When the entire complex of muscles around the facial orifices (mouth, nose and eyes) is involved, movement of those orifices is upward producing an expression of joy and contentment. Thus the popular saying: "Elevate the corners of your mouth and elevate your mood".

When a smile is forced, faked or artificial it only uses the muscles around the mouth and cheeks. A genuine smile, on the other hand, will also involve the muscles around the eyes. One cannot command the eye muscles to smile; only an authentic smile can mobilize those upper face groups of muscles. Using this non-verbal signal, you can easily determine if someone's smile is fake or authentic.

Figure 21: Authentic smile (left) and forced smile (right)
Notice the muscles around the eyes that are not involved in the forced smile.

In the second half of the nineteenth century, the father of human physiognomy, Duchenne de Boulogne[31], asserted: *"The soul is the source of emotional expression, which activates facial muscles and shapes them into the characteristic forms of our passion"*.

His goal in studying physiognomy was to discover the emotional make up of a subject by observing facial expression; judging the "inside by the outside". Ekman[32] later confirmed the universality of facial expression as communication through multi-cultural studies.

Those who studied smile physiognomy describe the following stages of a smile: pre-smile, tempered smile, open smile and broad smile.

These successive stages involve different groups of muscles and are triggered by different emotional states. Smiling is such a complex anatomical and psycho-physiological phenomenon, yet is so touching in its simplicity.

Illustrations of the phases of a smile

Figure 22: Tempered smile

Physiology and Function of a Smile

Illustrations of the phases of a smile

Figure 23: Pre-smile

Figure 24: Open smile

Figure 25: Broad smile

Heart-Smiling

Electromagnetic Fields and Smiling

Every cell and organism is bathed in the electromagnetic (em) field it generates. The em spectrum encompasses a wide variety of forces, ranging from cosmic rays to radio waves, including visual and auditory frequencies. The sun and earth each have their own overlapping em field.

In the same manner, the heart and the brain are under each other's em influence. As seen previously, the heart possesses em activity 50 times greater than the brain, which can be measured up to 15 feet outside the body. The shape of this em field is a giant doughnut, or torus, that surrounds the entire body. Earth also has her own em field we are all bathed in, and it is possible to align our personal em field with that of the earth, for example, during worldwide meditations.

When two people are close to each other physically, they penetrate each other's em field and can perceive the other's "vibration". Even animals pick out the emotional charge inscribed in this field. If someone is afraid, an animal will detect it. Even though animals do not smile, they are "smile sensitive" and sense the emotional vibration of our em field. Victor Hugo said: *"A dog smiles with his tail"*.

Physiology and Function of a Smile

Smiling is associated with heart-felt emotions: joy, happiness, satisfaction, appreciation, gratitude, affection and compassion. A smile can be felt without visual contact. It can be sensed over the phone or by a blind person.

As mentioned earlier, smiling is crucial in parent-child bonding and plays an important role in the child's socialization. The overlapping of the smiling caregiver's em field with the child in his arm is, to some degree, responsible for that bonding influence.

Smiles are contagious. If you run across someone on the street or in a corridor and smile, you will usually trigger a responsive smile. Smiles are very powerful when issued from the heart; even overwhelmed people are lifted up by a genuine smile. Smiles are difficult to resist.

Smiles are contagious...

Functions of a Smile

1. Smiling Bonds Hearts

The newborn unknowingly uses its reflex smile as a powerful bonding device. When associated with cries, smiling helps keep Mom close by. Bonding between baby and mother (part of both their genetic programming) insures the survival of the specie. When a baby smiles, parents are captivated, hearts melt and an indestructible bond is formed.

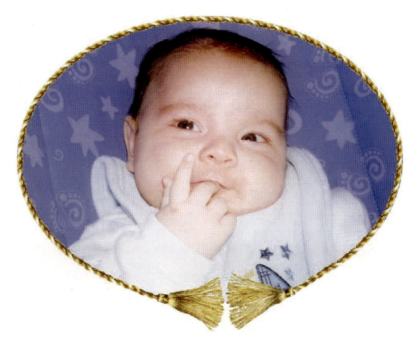

Figure 26: *The first function of a smile is to bond hearts.*

Physiology and Function of a Smile

Children learn to use smiling to get what they want, and adults have a hard time resisting. As time goes by, smiling takes on other forms, i.e., innocent, mischievous or cajoling.

Later in life, after puberty and during adulthood, smiles can become flirtatious and seductive.

Figure 27: *Mischievous smile*

Figure 28: *Seductive smile*

Mature adults use a "Conscious Smile" to touch, inspire and to show understanding, wisdom and compassion. This Conscious Smile is the smile from the heart that can transform our relationships and the world in which we live.

Figure 29: *"Conscious Smile" from the heart*

2. Smiling as a Means of Communication

Human communication depends on an assortment of signals, both simple and complex. Humans transmit universally recognizable signals through their physiognomy, which take only a few seconds to assess. In this way, we know what is about to happen before the first word is uttered.

Figure 30: Smile to communicate

Facial expression transmits personality, state of mind and mental state. An open smile is one of the most explicitly welcomed and understood signals of human physiognomy.

Physiology and Function of a Smile

3. Smiles Reassure

Our reptilian brain makes us perceive someone walking toward us as a possible threat, and elicits a "fight or flight" reaction. However, the more evolved parts of our brain assess the situation and probe for signs of intention. Valuable information can be read in posture and facial expression.

An open smiling face is reassuring; it transmits peace and good intention. A humble authentic smile has the potential to disarm and radically transform the dynamic of an aggressive confrontation. A shut down, expressionless face makes us suspicious.

Figure 31: *A welcoming and reassuring smile reassures.*

Heart-Smiling

4. Pleasurable Smiles

Circulating endorphins, produce a sense of pleasure and well-being, and can generate a smile. It does not matter if the secretion of endorphins is triggered by a real situation, an imagined situation or a memory; when pleasure is felt, one smiles from satisfaction and/or appreciation.

Figure 32: *Smiles of pleasure*

4. Smiles of success and to look pretty

In our western world smiling is linked with success, wealth, health and beauty. Many people force an optimistic smile in order to transmit success.

It is a notorious fact that smiling makes people more attractive. The writer Claude Frisoni simply states: *"One has to smile to be pretty"*

Figure 33*: Smile to be pretty.*

Physiology and Function of a Smile

Catherine Gélinas, editorialist, writes: *"A smile is worth a thousand words: it can replace a word of encouragement, condolence or compliment. This facial expression invites complicity, gives pleasure, reassures and brings peace"*.

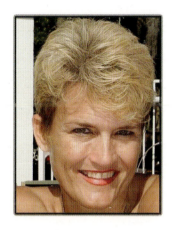

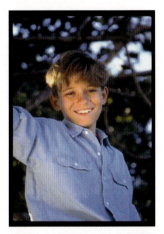

Figure 34: *A smile is worth a thousand words.*

In summary, Heart-Smiling is a coherence-inducing technique that synchronizes brain with heart. The resulting changes in internal chemistry and electromagnetic field influence our physiology and our perception of the world and experience.

Practicing this smile-inducing technique gives us the ability to change the non-verbal signals we send, increase the quality of interpersonal exchange, and temper our communication with respect, benevolence, understanding and empathy.

Practice of Heart-Smiling
⬇
Heart / Brain Synchronization
⬇
Transformation of internal climate
⬇
Changes in chemistry and electromagnetic field
⬇
New non-verbal signals
⬇
Transformation in perceptions and attitudes producing acceptance and respect
⬇
Improvement of the quality of life.

Table 6: *The practice of Heart-Smiling transforms lives.*

Section 3

Applications of Heart-Smiling to Personal Energy Management

Chapter 6

Seven Levels of Personal Energy

The first step to managing personal energy is to understand our personal energy drives and energy drains. The different types of energy can be classified in many systems. The seven categories described in this model are derived from Maslow's[33] pyramid of basic needs and adapted from Richard Barrett's[34] seven levels of consciousness"

Four new categories: " energy of transformation", " energy of personal mastery", "leadership energy" and "public service energy" have been added to the standard classification of energy types (physical, emotional, and intellectual). All aspects of personal energy are intertwined and interconnected and have been classified here into seven distinct levels, which coincide with the seven oriental energy centers called chakras.

The graphic representation of the Seven Levels of Personal Energy model is presented in Table 7. Although the graphic representation of the seven levels is vertical there is no value judgment intended; there are no superior or inferior levels.

The human energy structure is made up of seven different types of energy and are the "stuff" of which we are made. We are using energy all the time, even when sleeping. Every activity uses a different aspect of our energy pool. Becoming aware of the level of energy activated in every situation is the key to better personal energy management. We need to understand situational energy and learn how to consciously direct it to create and maintain harmony for our own benefit and for the benefit of those around us.

One needs to love and respect the body and give it what it needs to function optimally. Knowing what to do or what to avoid in order to replenish our energy, is often not enough. Knowledge of the right foods and right exercises is often not a strong enough stimulus to entice us to engage in energy-providing activities. Most of us need an extra factor to make us excited about helping ourselves. This indispensable extra factor is *self-love*. Only after the ability to access the power of self-love is learned and established is personal energy management possible.

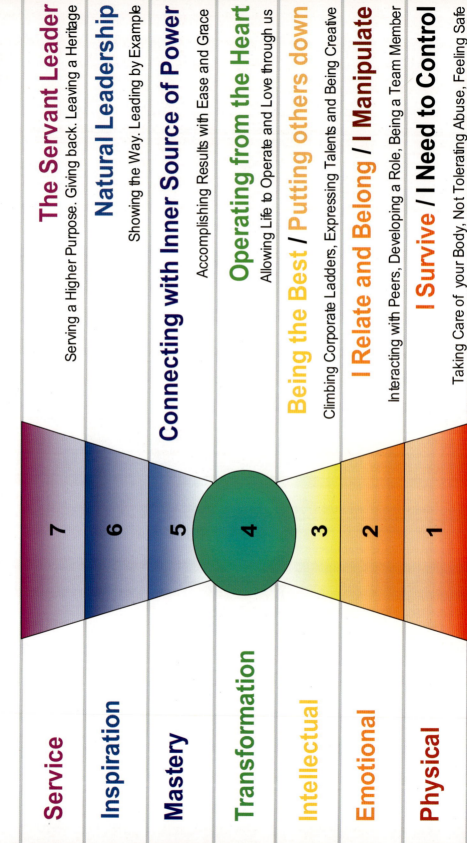

Heart-Smiling is the perfect tool for achieving the shift from energy depletion to energy abundance. Let's see how Heart-Smiling can help in managing each energy level.

I- Physical Energy: basic survival energy level.

In order for the human species to survive, it needs food, shelter, and care (if wounded or sick). Humans also need to reproduce, which involves dealing with sexual energy.

Each body has its own specific energy requirements. One must start by first identifying ones own body type and internal biorhythms.

> *MaryAnn and Bob met at work and have been living together for 3 years. They share many ideas about life, are passionate about the same issues, embrace the same causes. They can stay up and discuss politics or the last movie they saw for hours. However, they have a problem: they do not seem to be able to agree on leisure time activities to enjoy together, other than the movies. She is an early riser and enjoys running and kayaking. He is a night owl and prefers racket sports or team games.*

Some people are sprinters, others are long distance runners: different paces and different energy types. Bob and MaryAnn are a typical example of people who do not have the same internal rhythms. They always feel out of sync, constantly adjusting to each other. This requires effort and feels unnatural. This kind of relationship implies a complicated energy drain.

Applications of Heart-Smiling to Personal Energy Management

Biological clocks are not all set at the same time and biological cycles (linked to cortisol production cycles) are different for every individual. If hormonal blood levels were to be measured in Bob and MaryAnn at different times during the day, huge individual variations would be observed, which explains the variations in their respective energy cycles and life-style choices.

Humans are all responsible for the fulfillment of their own specific physical needs. It would be interesting if each one of us would ask ourselves the following questions many times during the day:
• What and when should I eat?
• When should I go to sleep and for how long?
• What type of exercise or leisure activity should I do?

One has to choose and prioritize. Modern life will impose its crazy pace and make life impossible if one doesn't have enough self-love and self-respect to identify the body's basic needs and prioritize them.

To prioritize self-care is not selfish. On the contrary, if one works his or her body into an optimal physical state, one will be healthier and live longer, and also have enough energy to be able to help others more and longer. A tired, overworked, abused body can only become a source of problems. Everyone around will benefit from ones ability to take the best possible care of ones physical self.

Often, because of outdated family programming, taking care of our own needs is considered egoistic. A mother feels she has to attend to her children and husband's need before her own. New fathers also feel they have to give up their lives to raise their families. Sacrificing parents are often honored in our culture. "Selfish" action is considered shameful.

One needs to learn to say "No" to other people's needs gently but firmly when they conflict with ones own. For example, declining ill-timed invitations, or refusing that other drink is part of learning to love oneself enough to make health and well being ones biggest priority. When tired and energy depleted, it is impossible to give the best of oneself. When we lovingly cares for ourselves consciously, we strengthen the possibility of being able to care for others more effectively.

Practicing Heart-Smiling to increase personal energy is very powerful because it taps into the power of self-love, making us put our needs first.

Those who learn to prioritize their needs to manage their personal energy are available for people they love.

> *Compassion is not only for other, but should be directed to self. Self-compassion is beneficial to health.*
> Dalaï Lama

HEART-SMILING: TAP INTO THE POWER OF SELF-LOVE AND INCREASE PHYSICAL ENERGY

1. Bring your attention to your heart and breathe effortlessly from the center of your chest. Become aware of your thoughts, feelings and sensations. Identify any discomfort. Scan your body in search for areas needing your attention.

2. Focus again on breathing from the heart. Bring a situation where you experienced bursting energy, stamina, and radiant health to your awareness. Experience those emotions, right now, again and surrender to the warm pleasant feeling this exercise generates. **Feel the loving flow of energy from your heart permeating each of your cells.** Let a smile come to your lips.

3. Pay attention to the changes that may be taking place in your body. Take advantage of this heart connection and **ask your heart for suggestions about how to increase the quality of your physical energy.** Be determined to follow through on what is revealed to you.

The Need to Control

Survival energy deals with food supply, shelter, physical safety and integrity. The need to control comes from feeling threatened at any energy level and is a survival mechanism related to an archaic need to control a hostile environment. This was ingrained in our programming since we slithered among the undergrowth on our reptilian bellies. Every time one feels threatened, the need to control resurfaces as a defense mechanism.

When the threat of loss is perceived in personal and work relationships, the need to control pops up its ugly head. Ugly because, when the loss is not related to survival, the need to control becomes an inappropriate over-reaction and creates problems. Trying to control the uncontrollable (other people and outside situations) uses an incredible amount of energy, time and resources and it is totally inefficient at avoiding the dreaded loss most of the time.

> *When John married Sally, she already had a serious drinking problem. But he thought that by surrounding her with love and providing a stable life, things would get better and she wouldn't need to drink as much. When he realized that this was not happening, he tried to control her drinking. He proceeded to hide the bottles and mark the level of liquid to check the quantities she was drinking. He refused invitations where he knew drinking would be involved and stopped inviting friends home in order to avoid the embarrassment of having his wife intoxicated in public.*

Applications of Heart-Smiling to Personal Energy Management

Despite all those control strategies, the drinking kept progressing, as Sally became an expert at outsmarting him. Her need for a drink was stronger than his ability to control her. John spent a lot of energy trying to control his wife's drinking. One day he finally admitted his inability to control her behavior and accepted help at learning new and healthier coping mechanisms.

Control, as a defense mechanism, drains energy and attains very poor long-term results. Control-based strategies, widely used in totalitarian countries and dictatorships, are universally unsuccessful in modern societies where individual freedom has become a fundamental right.

Sexual Energy: the need to procreate for the survival of the species.

The need for strong males to protect the family is a genetically imposed theme in human relationships. Sexual energy is linked to hormonal production: testosterone in males, and estrogen, progesterone and oxytocin in females. In the evolutionary cycle, our mammalian predecessors have defined the roles of sexual hormones. In males, testosterone promotes physical stamina and creates a biological need to conquer and inseminate. Feminine hormones insure fertility and receptivity to semen during periods of fertility.

In humans, gender roles have taken a specific direction because mothers and babies experience a very long period of vulnerability, as human offspring become autonomous very slowly. The need for strong males to protect them has been part of our survival skills for millennia.

Human behaviors retained by evolution to preserve the species are:
- women show signs of fertility;
- men conquer and inseminate;
- men protect and provide;
- women feed and raise children.

Gender roles have some biological basis. Women seduce and men conquer. Testosterone-driven men need to conquer, while hormone-driven women need to "keep their men". Complementary hormone-driven roles have allowed the disadvantaged human species to survive despite its overwhelmingly vulnerable status.

These behaviors have not adapted to the needs of modern life, where physical strength is no longer an indicator of survival ability. With the development of contraception, sperm banks and DNA testing, traditional father roles are being painstakingly questioned by society.

At the beginning of the 20th century, 94% of North American families lived on farms. During WW II, traditional gender roles started to shift as women were asked to support the war effort by working in food, clothing, supplies and weapons factories.

Today, both mothers and fathers share the role of provider in most homes and fathers are taking a more and more active role in child upbringing. Gender roles are being redefined based on need and possibility and are not necessarily compatible with biological urge.

It is difficult to reconcile sexual drive, ingrained thousands of years ago, with modern needs that became apparent less than a hundred years ago. Old deep programming is hard to erase! Managing sexual energy has become an art. Everyone needs to learn to master it in order to stop being dominated by sexual urges.

Sexual education has become necessary to teach teens not to confuse sexual drive with love. Teenagers and young adults are being taught to become aware that "hormones talk". The decision to get married or to live together is still often based on unsatisfied sexual or emotional needs. This has created generations of relationships where painful breakups have become the norm.

The average length of marriage in the USA is seven years. Learning to use criteria other than sexual compatibility and emotional need when choosing a partner is the only way to change this sad statistic. Shared values and compatible priorities have a better chance of leading to harmonious relationships. However, the benefits of sexual energy are still very important.

Sexual energy can powerfully sustain love-based relationships. Well-channeled sexual energy is a tremendous bonding force: it epitomizes the drive for fusion, the yearning to become one. Oxytocin, the "hormone of love", is secreted by the heart and the brain during lovemaking and is liberated in the blood flow after orgasm. This definitely contributes to the strengthening of relationships.

Learning to identify and manage sexual energy is a double blessing because, not only, you are no longer controlled by it, but you can use this tremendous bonding energy to create loving and enduring relationships.

Seven Levels of Personal Energy

HEART-SMILING: BALANCE YOUR SEXUAL ENERGY

1. Bring your attention to your heart and breathe effortlessly from the center of your chest. Become aware of your thoughts, emotions and the quality of your sexual energy.

2. Focus again on breathing from the heart. Bring to your consciousness a memory of a situation where you experienced intense, free-flowing and well-balanced sexual energy. **Feel awe and respect for the power of the Life force surging through you.** Experience those feelings again, right now, and surrender to this powerful energy. Let a smile come to your lips.

3. Pay attention to the changes that are taking place in your body and your sexual energy levels. Take advantage of this heart connection to **ask your Heart to guide you to the most appropriate ways** to harmonize and express this powerful life-supporting energy.

II- Emotional Energy: the need to belong, to create and sustain relationships. Family and community life are nurtured at this level.

Emotion is the power behind thought. Emotions cannot be classified as "positive" or "negative". Emotions just are. To deny, repress or ignore them creates severe consequences on physical and mental health and is a serious deterrent to enjoying life.

Fear, anger, rage, guilt and especially shame are vampires of energy. If allowed to proliferate in ones mindscape, they take over and contaminate the whole picture. However, it is *impossible* to shield oneself from only painful emotion. In doing so, one inevitably obstructs the feeling of the healthy pleasant emotions, like joy, happiness, enthusiasm, etc. Disconnecting from emotion clips ones wings and extinguishes the fire that ignites the manifestation process of ones dreams. Emotion makes us feel alive. Without emotion, we are like robots.

> *I always felt exhausted when I was an intern. I remember saying that my only support was the coffee machine in the OR. Life was very dull in those days. Nothing excited me.*
>
> *On one of those rare Sunday afternoons off, a friend dragged me to a nearby frozen lake where people were ice fishing. As we approached a group of fishermen, one had just caught a fish and was unhooking his line. This scene made me grimace with pain. The sight of a mutilated fish repulsed me. The fisherman, seeing my face, said:" Miss, you would definitely not be a good nurse".*

His remark hit me like a hammer. In my hospital, I was known as the most efficient of ER interns, precisely because I was able to bury my emotions and not let them impair my judgment or my decision-making. I thought I had mastered the art of suppressing my emotions; and there I was, weeping over a little fish! This came to me as a revelation: I still had emotions! All those years of medical training had failed to completely suppress my ability to feel.

Emotions are not negative, but how one deals with them, may have negative or positive consequences. It is essential to acknowledge and identify ones emotions. Being able to step back and observe emotion enables one to choose the appropriate behavioral response to any given situation. Learning to express emotion in a loving way requires a close evaluation of habitual emotional reactions. In order to stimulate harmony, one must learn how to express emotion appropriately and never be abusive to oneself or to others.

Emotional detachment is key. One needs to be able to detach from the situation and learn to see oneself as actor and director on the stage of life. Becoming an observer in a stressful situation enables us to consider an endless array of available scripts. Why not choose one with a happy ending?

Like an actor, one needs to learn and practice a vast repertoire of behavioral reactions adapted to various scenarios. By adding new roles and practicing them, we become skillful at appropriate responses in emotional situations. It is very limiting to be confined to one emotional reaction to a given situation. *"Those with only a hammer see nails everywhere"*. If one fills ones tool box with many different tools and learns to use them, life becomes easier and more fun!

Applications of Heart-Smiling to Personal Energy Management

In order to learn to respond rather than react, it is necessary to develop the ability to detach from the emotional charge of a situation. This detachment allows one to withhold the impulse to react long enough to consider and respond in a more appropriate manner.

Emotions contain a fabulous potential for creativity. Artistic inspiration and expression is emotion-based. Great artists have proven this over and over again. Difficult emotions, although often hard to handle, may be powerful sources of creativity. Some very disturbed artists, like Vincent Van Gogh, have produced great works of arts.

Difficult emotions can be transformed into allies. However they must evolve from repressed to accepted to integrated in order to become available to us.

"Queen Fury"

I once took a week's vacation at the seaside and read a self-help book. It suggested, "at this point, if you felt any emotions surfacing, put down the book and try to identify the emotion". I followed the recommendation while pacing on the beach. The emotion that came up was a volcano of rage located in the lower part of my abdomen and ready to erupt.

My first reaction was to put the lid back on this 'can of worms' and walk away from it; but a 'little voice inside' suggested differently. I gathered enough courage to have a second look at this red fiery monster living inside me. After being able to tolerate its stare for a few minutes, the same 'little voice' suggested I have a conversation with the monster. I gave it a name: "Queen Fury", and proceeded to ask her a few questions: Who

are you? What do you want from me? She said she was my anger and that mostly, she wanted to be heard. Like children, emotions are trying to get our attention mostly out of a need to be heard rather than to be right.

I knew that I was dealing with a very powerful destructive force, so I decided to make a pact with her: "Every time you want to tell me something, I promise that I will listen; but in return, I expect you to consult with me each time before you act out". Since that time, I have never acted out angrily: I listen to what she wants to bring to my attention and we always agree on a non-violent intervention.

When facing abusive situations, I know I can count on her strength and powerful energy to dispose of any aggressor. "Queen Fury" has been transformed from potentially destructive rage into a powerful protector. She is no longer this unconscious, dark and troubling force, ready to erupt without notice. She is now my powerful ally and guard, always ready to defend me if needed.

The appropriate use of anger is to give the courage and physical strength to stop abuse. Anger helps muster the force and courage to put our foot down and say: "Stop! Enough!" It sends a very clear message: abuse will not be tolerated!

I invite you to stop seeing anger or rage as 'negative' and realize these emotions can be very helpful when used appropriately. There are no positive or negative emotions, only appropriate and inappropriate ways to express them.

Applications of Heart-Smiling to Personal Energy Management

EMOTIONAL MANIPULATION

1. Manipulative Persuasion

Since the beginning of time, emotions have been used to manipulate. The purpose of emotional manipulation is to persuade someone to do something considered vital or useful. Fear, guilt and shame are usually the emotions involved in this type of abusive strategy.

Powerless parents manipulate their children when they use these phrases: *"Shame on you!" "You ought to be ashamed of yourself." "After all I did for you, this is the least you could do for me." "Who do you think you are?" "Wait until your father comes back!"*

Political leaders use fear to manipulate their public. Hitler, for instance, misled the German people into believing that war was the only option to protect Germany from the perceived threat of French power.

In a similar manner, religious leaders of all times have used fear and guilt to control and secure their "flock". Many wars have been fought on the pretext of exterminating "evil", when in fact, power and territory or financial gain were the real issues.

"Celestine Prophecies", by James Redfield illustrates how people's energy can be manipulated and diverted to benefit someone's need for attention or appreciation. Redfield also emphasizes that becoming aware of those 'games' is the first step to preventing these energy leaks.

2. Retaliation

Another example of emotional manipulation is the need to get even, to retaliate. Retaliation can include behaviors like refusing to communicate verbally or even sexually. The 'silent treatment' is an exasperating strategy used to try and punish someone for not behaving according to the expectations of others. When applied, the silent treatment leaves a dark cloud of pending doom over the entire ambience and drains the energy of everyone around including innocent victims like children.

3. Resentment

Resentment is yet another inappropriately manipulative expression of anger. Resentment is similar to poisoning oneself in hopes someone else will die. To entertain resentment is to "volunteer for martyrdom". This self-punishing attitude drains a lot of energy. Resentment usually only hurts the person resenting because it is a passive form of demonstrating anger and the target is often not aware there is a problem.

4. Shame

Shame is the most painful of all emotions. It is the 'cancer of the soul' that devours a person from the inside out. Feeling ashamed, unworthy and deficient is, again, passive and rarely affects someone else.

There is a huge difference between shame and guilt. Shame is much more devastatingly painful. To explain the difference, we will use the analogy of a football field. Guilt comes from doing something wrong and can be wiped away by paying a penalty. Shame comes from not feeling good enough and can only melt away by increasing self-esteem.

Applications of Heart-Smiling to Personal Energy Management

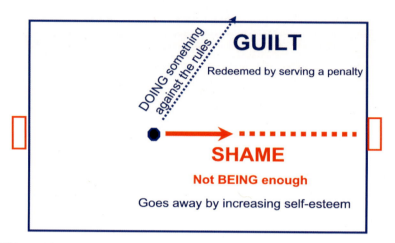

When a player kicks the ball outside of the field, he gets a penalty for breaking a rule. Once he pays the penalty, the player can resume the game emotionally debt-free. If on the other hand, at a critical moment in the game he misses the goal and his team loses, the prevailing emotion is not guilt but shame. This player will feel terrible and probably see himself as a failure, not good enough. Shame is always connected with self-perception. There is no penalty for missing a goal and, therefore, no way to redeem oneself. The only way one can stop feeling shame is by working on ones self-perception and self-esteem

Support Groups

Support groups are one of the best self-esteem builders available to Western Society today. It is impossible to 'inject' someone with self-esteem. Participants in support groups learn to value themselves through the eyes of their peers. Peers listen to each other and, after a time, start taking each other more seriously. Just the act of having someone listen to ones problems and make empathic comments progressively builds ones self-esteem. Eventually, participants learn to see themselves as worthy of respect and love. Support groups like Co-Dependant Anonymous are especially useful when emotional manipulation is affecting relationships.

Emotional Intelligence

In his book "Emotional Intelligence"[6], Daniel Goleman cleverly addresses the topic of emotional energy management. One of his operational definitions of emotional intelligence (EQ) is *"the ability to sense, understand and effectively apply the power and acumen of emotions as a source of human energy, information, connection and influence"*.

Goleman insists on the intrinsic neutral quality of emotions, which are neither positive nor negative. Contrary to IQ, which reaches a ceiling after age 25, EQ can be developed at any age. One can always learn to manage ones emotions more effectively and benefit from related health advantages.

---

6 STEPS TO MANAGING YOUR EMOTIONS

1. Identify the emotion. *"I'm scared."*

2. Understand the emotional unfoldment: what are the triggers and the extinguishers. *"What am I afraid of? What triggered this fear? What can I do to stop feeling this fear"*

3. Practice detachment: switch to your observer-self. *"I am more than my emotions; I produce them and can learn to manage them"*

4. Practice empathy: develop the ability to feel what others feel. *"What is he/she afraid of?"*

5. Express your emotions in a healthy and loving way. *"I feel ...." " I am sorry you are in pain"*

6. Use the creative power of emotions to improve the quality of your life.

Tapping into the Power of Emotions

Emotions are powerful tools. They transform ideas into action, dreams into reality. To repress emotion is to deprive oneself from the greatest drive for accomplishment available.

Emotions are the source of personal power, motivation, influence and manifestation of dreams. In order to experience a life worth living, it is mandatory to learn to use the emotions of the heart like intuition, passion, enthusiasm as creative power.

One must stop being constantly driven by fear of rejection or the need for approval. The consequence of these beliefs is a fearful powerless existence.

> Emotions are the POWER behind your Thoughts

The Need to be Right

Have you ever seen teams competing at "Tug of War"? The winners are those who pull harder in order to cross the line first. When people have an escalating argument, they play "Tug of War". They each 'tug' vehemently trying to prove their point.

Needing to be right is very costly in terms of energy, especially if it causes long drawn out conflict. Stop pulling and drop the rope. This is the most intelligent, astute way to save ones personal energy and throws the opponent immediately off balance sending a clear message that one does not want to play this game.

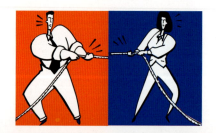

The underlying attitude: "I would rather be happy than right", is an energy saver that takes the protagonists to another level of relating where they can "agree to disagree". "Dropping the rope" is the respectful way of dealing with situations that drain energy. Everyone feels relieved.

Blame

Holding others responsible for ones problems and difficulties is another energy black hole. When one blames, one gives power away and gives another person the power to make one miserable. The key principle of mature emotional management is that nobody can make someone else happy or miserable, only *YOU* have this power!

Blaming is an unskillful attempt to control one's life and it doesn't work. To put ones source of power outside of oneself is a mistake. Power, like happiness, comes from within. Blaming blocks one from ones real source of power. The following phrases are examples of looking for the power to change experience 'in all the wrong places: *"If you really loved me, you would treat me differently." "Change your behavior because I'm in pain." "I hurt because of you."*

Emotional pain is the result of interpretation and has to be "bought into". Everyone has the choice of how to read and understand a situation. Because emotions belong to the person experiencing them, pain does also.

The perception of a situation determines its emotional charge, not the situation itself. Different people experience the same situation differently. If someone is accused of being stupid or ugly, the accused has the choice of believing this assertion or not. Ones reaction and

Applications of Heart-Smiling to Personal Energy Management

belief will be based on whether one agrees with the accuser or not. Emotional pain is based on the fear, guilt, and shame one harbors, not on the words of others.

Unless physical constraint is involved, someone else's behavior can only affect us if we make the decision to give this behavior that power. Some people are always late, for example. This can negatively affect someone who interprets this behavior as a sign of disrespect or rejection, while another person in the same situation might just walk away after waiting a few minutes and not feel offended.

> EMOTIONAL PAIN IS ALWAYS SELF-INFLICTED
> BY ONES OWN INTERPRETATIONS

Tolerating Abusive Situations Drains Loads of Energy

Do not tolerate any situation that involves emotional abuse. Tolerating abuse demonstrates a lack of self-love and self-respect and is extremely costly energy wise. Abuse of any type is best dealt with by denouncing it, by talking about it to people you trust. Remove yourself from the abusive situation, leave the room. It is very important to set very clear limits about what is acceptable and what is not. Also announce the consequences should the abuse start again or should those limits be transgressed. The difficult part, where support is often needed, is to follow through with the consequences. Failing to follow through makes you come across as a whiner, someone who is only complaining but is not serious about having limits respected.

Seven Levels of Personal Energy

Tolerating abuse is often linked to past programming, which can always be changed. Past experiences can influence ones present patterns of behavior and may not be appropriate to the present situation. People who are raised in families where there is a verbal abuse, for example, may have a tendency to shout and scream whenever there is a need to communicate. This person learned to communicate in his family, but, later on in life it will be necessary to relearn more appropriate skills.

Dr. Boris Cyrulnik[36] is a French neuro-psychiatrist who wrote extensively on the resilience of severely traumatized war children. He says: *"Unfortunately in our culture, abused children are guided on the path of 'victimhood"*. He defines resilience as "the ability to navigate in torrents". He has found that resilient children who lived through horrific situations can still choose not to wear the asphyxiating garment of the victim and lead healthy happy lives.

> **WE CAN ALWAYS CHOOSE OUR PERCEPTIONS AND REACTIONS TO ANY SITUATION**

The secret to an emotionally rich life is to free oneself from restrictive past programming and to learn to choose emotional responses appropriately. In order to avoid emotional energy leaks, one needs to see oneself as the decision maker. One of the crucial decision to make in life is choosing between being happy or being a victim. Quality of life is based on the decision to take responsibility for personal experience. This implies choosing the right emotional responses in any given situation.

Applications of Heart-Smiling to Personal Energy Management

HEART-SMILING: REDIRECT EMOTIONAL ENERGY FROM FEAR TO LOVE

1. Bring your attention to your heart and breathe effortlessly from the center of your chest. Become aware of your thoughts, feelings and sensations. Identify any discomfort.

2. Focus again on breathing from the heart. Bring to your memory a person or a situation that made your heart "sing". It could be a moment of immense joy, gratitude, profound peace, touching love or compassion. **Experience those higher emotions** again, right now, and surrender to the warm pleasant feeling in your heart. **Let a smile come to your lips.**

3. Pay attention to the changes that are taking place in your body. Note any change in attitude and perception. If you are dealing with a fearful situation, take advantage of this heart connection to ask your heart to guide you to a **loving solution**.

Learn Self-Motivation: Change Inappropriate Behaviors

Changing undesirable behavior is not easy. We hold on to "bad habits" because they are familiar. Our old programming brings survival strategies to the surface, which we learned in our family of origin during traumatic situations. We keep repeating these survival behaviors in adulthood, even though they are not appropriate anymore.

Lying, for example, is a behavior adopted in childhood as a protection against consequences of telling the truth, which are perceived as terrifying: "My father would kill me if he knew the truth." Some adults use compulsive lying as an automatic defense mechanism, even when lying is no longer required for protection from an abusive father. For one to change such self-defeating behavior, one must first want to change. This motivation to change comes from understanding the advantages of changing old patterns.

Motivation can be based on fear, anticipation of reward or personal values. Results depend on the type of motivation: the stick or the carrot.

Fear, Guilt or Shame-based Motivation

Fear, Guilt and Shame are very effective motivators. Tyrants of all kinds have successfully used these to acquire and maintain power or financial gain. Negative motivation however, can be helpful in situations where consequences could become disastrous, like when we spend the weekend studying in order not to fail an exam or pay taxes in order not to go to jail.

Reward-based Motivation

Reward-based motivation techniques, seemingly more appealing, are often not very efficient for deep-rooted behavioral change, particularly in the case of addictive behaviors. The attractiveness of the reward has to be increased with each positive result attained in order to maintain its enticement value. If you motivate a teenager to clean his room with money, for example, expect to have to raise him regularly to keep him motivated.

Value-based Motivation

The most powerful way to motivate people is by touching their hearts with inspiring values. Instilling pride, fostering generosity and inviting people to make a difference are very powerful ways to motivate and inspire them.

When respect is an important value, one can draw on self-respect to change unhealthy habits and to treat oneself in a respectful way.

> **THE SECRET TO EFFICIENT PERSONAL ENERGY MANAGEMENT IS TO LOVE AND RESPECT ONESELF AND TO ACT ACCORDINGLY.**

III- Intellectual Energy

Curiosity and creativity are both elements of Mental Energy. Intellectual values motivate accoé41mplishments and lead us to success. At some point in everyone's development, being the best and proving one's worth becomes imperative.

> *Henry came from an underprivileged family. Thanks to his clear focus and superior intelligence, he completed University. Inspired by his need to make a difference and to alleviate pain, he opted for medical school, to which his exceptional intelligence and grades gave him access. After post-graduate studies at a prestigious medical center, he became one of the youngest and most brilliant surgeons of his generation. At 40, he was 'the best'. He had a brilliant career, notoriety and financial success, everything a prominent medical career can offer.*

Successes and accomplishments are important in personal development because they instill self-confidence. A necessary phase in personal growth, performance and excellence generate recognition and self-esteem. Unfortunately, for 90% of us, growth stops after reaching the top rung of the ladder. For others, it takes many ladders before one considers oneself worthy. Still others never get there.

After climbing the perceived ladder to success, people are often disappointed. As Joseph Campbell pointed out, *"there is nothing more depressing than to realize, after climbing all the way to the top of the ladder, that you have placed your ladder against the wrong wall"*.

Career crises are common for those who have reached their goals. Successful people often feel they made a mistake or chose the wrong path when they reach their goals. Passion and purposefulness are often missing after the attainment of a summit. There is a shocking uncertainty in the face of this new void that past excellence cannot fill. Those who have the courage to quest onward to find the missing ingredients are the lucky ones.

The Need to Put Others Down

The down side of 'being the best' is that a person so motivated often needs to put others down in order to look and feel better. Many low self-esteemed persons use this strategy to get ahead.

> *Peter was part of middle management in his organization and believed he could only improve his position within the company by 'eliminating the competition', i.e., all those who had the potential to get the advancement he wanted. All his energy was spent proving to his superiors that the other managers were unsuited for targeted promotions. Clearly, Peter did not have many friends. The price he had to pay for his undermining competitive style was the ostracizing of distrustful colleagues.*

Paternalism

Paternalism is another control mechanism at the intellectual level. This one-up-one-down attitude prompted certain leaders and other authority figures to control information "for the good of the children". This form of abuse of power has been used since the beginning of recorded history. Leaders think and decide. Followers comply.

Restricting information maintains ignorance and creates a state of intellectual infantilism in a targeted population that, as a result, becomes more easily controlled. "All truth is not good to be divulged" is often used to control people and rob their intellectual energy, their ability to do their own thinking.

In his essay on "Self-Reliance", Ralph Waldo Emerson exhorts his readers to look closely at each idea and assess its relevance before including it in their belief system. Beliefs acquired during childhood must be challenged throughout ones lifetime. It is inappropriate to defend ones beliefs based only on historical validity. In order to be currently beneficial, beliefs need to be reassessed in adulthood.

This conscious reassessment allows the believer to become the "owner" of his/her beliefs. When people do not "own" their beliefs, they are often confused, fearful and defensive as a result. These behavior traits often put them in conflict with the world around them, further deepening their feelings of insecurity. If there is no congruence between what one thinks, says and does, one cannot "walk the talk". These people often seek dogma and group support to allay their fears rather than opening up to the reality of change.

In order to self-manage intellectual energy, one needs to be vigilant and monitor ones thoughts. Never let someone else impose beliefs, choices and decisions. Stay intellectually alert, read, participate in book clubs, join a group that stimulates your curiosity and creativity, attend your local library activities, and volunteer to help children who will challenge your beliefs.

Intellectual laziness has ruined many careers and cut the wings of many artists. It is infinitely easier to rely on the research of others and to blindly accept third-party conclusions and recommendations. However, this careless way of acquiring new information produces gullible masses easy to manipulate.

Intellectual laziness allows others to inform, guide and influence our decisions. Every marketing and political campaign is based on intellectual laziness and gullibility. Political and religious leaders count on the willingness of their flock to relinquish their power to think and feverishly study complex techniques of stimulating the trust required for such surrender.

Applications of Heart-Smiling to Personal Energy Management

For decisions regarding their health, patients tend to rely on health professionals to inform them and allow these outside elements to make important decisions on their behalf. Patients neglect collecting their own information about the nature of their diseases and different treatment possibilities.

Thoroughly researching ones own condition allows a patient to become an expert on his/her case. Doctors and health professionals should be used as consultants and become valued partners. Many of them have years of experience and intelligence-based beliefs.

Involvement puts the responsibility of ones own treatment onto ones own shoulders. Positioning oneself as the expert and decision maker eliminates the possibility of being a victim of mismanagement.

When it is time to make a decision regarding your treatment, be the decision maker. It is your health, your life. Patients, take charge! As a patient, you are encouraged to gather information, consult specialists, discuss the case with peers and finally, rely on the wisdom of the Heart to make treatment choices.

For low back pain, for example, one needs to first gather information by reading and researching causes and available solutions. Some solutions involve health professionals. Others are ergonomic and deal with posture, which can be corrected with appropriate work chairs, better support shoes or a better quality mattress.

Next, one must select the correct health professional for each specific type of lower back pain condition. A general practitioner will diagnose and treat the problem with muscle relaxants and/or anti-inflammatory medication. A neurosurgeon is needed if the diagnosis requires the removal or replacement of an inter-vertebral disk. If only spinal manipulation is required, a chiropractor can do that. Physical therapists relieve inflammation and tension, and re-educate muscles. Massage therapists soothe tense muscles and bring comfort.

One must research and find the strengths and weaknesses of each therapeutic approach, get references from people who have successfully used them and evaluate all this input in relation to the problem.

The third step is deciding on the treatment option that best fits the present situation and should involve Heart intuition. There is usually only one appropriate solution for each individual situation at any given time and Heart intelligence knows which one that is. Brain intelligence finds possible options, but Heart intelligence chooses the right one.

Applications of Heart-Smiling to Personal Energy Management

Heart-based decision-making can be successfully applied to other personal and/or work related situations. In order for mental energy to flow optimally, we must exercise the intellect. It is just like toning a muscle. If you don't use it, you lose it. It is too precious to be wasted.

HEART-SMILING: WISE DECISION-MAKING

1. Bring your attention to your heart and breathe effortlessly from the center of your chest. Become aware of your thoughts, feelings and sensations. Identify any discomfort.

2. Focus again on breathing form your heart. Bring a success story where you felt good about trusting your intuition to your consciousness. Experience the feelings you felt then again, right now, and let a smile come to your lips.

3. Mentally review the different options available and present them to your Heart. **Ask your heart to show you the right solution.** Determine to follow through with what your heart reveals. Go forth with a feeling of confidence, enthusiasm and gratitude.

Enhancing the intellect with the intuitive powers of the heart comes also through practice and takes one closer to the primal desire of self-realization. Curiosity, alertness and creativity are intellectual functions that bloom in the light of self-respect and bear the fruit of self-realization.

IV- Energy of Heart Transformation

Heart energy transforms your experience. This energy level is pivotal in personal energy management. The Heart as decision maker taps into the wisdom and intuition of Universal Intelligence. It is necessary to go through the heart where there is no 'positive or negative' energy to access superior levels of personal experience.

With regard to physical, emotional and mental energy levels, we talked previously about change; changing habits, changing behaviors, changing attitudes. At the heart level, energy is about transformation.

> **CHANGE IS DOING THINGS DIFFERENTLY**
> **TRANSFORMATION IS BEING DIFFERENT**

Metamorphosis is a classic example of transformation. As the caterpillar becomes a butterfly, it takes on a new form, a new name, and a new identity. There is no personal effort required in transformation. Life force takes over and does the work. The caterpillar retreats into the cocoon and waits for transformation to occur.

Transformation is the motor of the self-actualization process. When an acorn becomes an oak, it transforms and expresses its potential. Likewise, people who go inside to their heart energy transform into the expression of their unique individual potential. Personal transformation requires seeing through the eyes of the Heart.

> *"Acorns grow into oaks, caterpillars grow into butterflies, and humans grow into God."*
> Anonymous

Applications of Heart-Smiling to Personal Energy Management

There is no effort or hard work needed for transformation. The only requirement is surrendering, allowing to be transformed by the life force that works its magic effortlessly. Flowers turn naturally to the sun. Branches grow effortlessly. Leaves fall softly. Babies grow without working at it. Humans grow in spite of consciousness. There is no need to struggle or work hard. Simply allow transformation to take place.

Life leaves clues. To know your unique potential and purpose on this planet, you must look at your passions and special talents. Once purpose is clear, all that is needed is to channel passion and transform this energy into a successful career and service to mankind.

The secret to a purposeful life is operating from the Heart. Joseph Chilton Pearce wrote: *"Once open to the heart, we recognize the Universe as benevolent and our personal self to be the center of that benevolence."* [37]

Life is like a rose garden or a candy store, where we choose the flowers or the candies we want. When we see life as being supportive, we can make personal use of that support to do whatever we want with our lives. The winds of creativity are blowing; it's up to us to raise our jib and sail into the life we want.

The moment we deny our heart a central role in decision-making, we lose contact with the power source, and it becomes impossible to create a fulfilling life expressing our magnificent potential. "Heart-Smiling" can unleash passions, help discover one's life purpose and help uncover creative means of expressing one's unique potential.

Seven Levels of Personal Energy

HEART-SMILING TO FOSTER PERSONAL GROWTH
FIND YOUR LIFE PURPOSE

1. Bring your attention to your heart and breathe effortlessly from the center of your chest. Become aware of your thoughts, feelings and sensations. Note your level of energy and feel the life force seeking expression through you. Examine your talents and passions. Look for your fire.

2. Focus again on breathing from the heart. Bring to your memory a situation where you experienced **passion, purposefulness,** and the **exhilaration of freely expressing your talents.** Experience those emotions again and surrender to the warm energy beginning to flow into your heart region. **Allow yourself to smile throughout your entire body.**

3. Pay attention to the changes that are taking place in your body, your attitude and your perception. Ask your heart to guide you to find **specific ways to express your unique potential in alignment with your life purpose**. Determine to follow through and to allow the life force to transform you in order to create a life filled with enthusiasm and generosity.

V- Energy of Mastery

In order to master ones life, one must acknowledge the existence of a non-physical dimension and give this spiritual (non-physical) aspect of human existence the central role. The spiritual dimension has to become the primary source of ones reality, the vital essence and life force. This life force must be seen as expressing through the human experience.

Mastery implies ease and precision of execution. Martial arts masters, for example, rely on life force as the driving force that moves them with each step of their art. However, spiritual energy, like physical and emotional energy, can be engulfed in existential black holes. Maladies of the soul: despair, hopelessness, uselessness, loneliness and isolation (to name only a few) are extremely painful. To cut oneself from spiritual energy is literally a death sentence, a condemnation to join the 'living-dead'.

An example of deep dissatisfaction with life is the famous "middle life crisis". Some people in their mid-thirties experience an acute awareness that youth is ephemeral. Its form is gender specific. Men experience an urgency to catch up with all the things they did not take the time to do while they were busy focusing on their careers. Lots of sports cars are sold to men at this age who look outside themselves for proof that they 'still have it' in terms of seductive power.

Women, on the other hand, experience the passage of youth as the threat of loosing the feminine attributes of motherhood and beauty. It is the 'my biological clock is ticking'-syndrome, or the 'empty nest'-syndrome, and the age of reconstructive plastic surgery.

To master life, trust the life force
expressing through you!

Existential crises are always spiritual in nature. "Carpe Diem" reminds us that life is short and that growing old is impossible to escape. The ability to transcend societal conditioning, which has transformed our natural human condition into some kind of pain-inducing monster, is embedded in our spiritual nature.

Most of us go through phases when we search for the meaning of existence. We spout woeful phrases like: *"There must be something more to life"* or *"I know I have a purpose to fulfill, I just don't know what yet"*. Cynical people affirm: *"Life is pointless: we live, then we die."* or *"Life is but an immense joke and the joke is on us!"*

Our *perception* of the world we live in creates a definite impact on our *experience*. If our perception is an unfriendly and hostile world ("they're out there to get me"), we become suspicious, helpless, powerless, cynical and resigned.

In order to change our experience of the world 'out there', one needs to change ones internal attitude towards it. The only way out of a spiritual crisis is to connect and relate with the deep intimate spiritual dimension.

The Way Out is the Way In

It is mandatory to maintain a spiritual connection to feel fully alive. Failing to take care of ones spirituality leads to chronic dissatisfaction, emptiness, bitterness, and eventual despair. One needs to believe in something greater than oneself and relate to it on a personal level for life to make sense.

Spirituality and religion are totally separate issues. Although the word religion comes from Latin "religare", which means to relate or have a relationship with, religions have changed into organizations based more on imposed dogma and belief systems than on relating. In belonging to a religion one must choose to live according to a set of values and code of ethics endorsed by this particular organization; in the same manner that one chooses political affiliations.

Spirituality, on the contrary, is highly individual and personal and is not necessarily linked to a group or a religious organization. Spirituality is an intimate alignment to higher Self where meaning and transcendence are personal and independent experiences. People today are opting more and more for being spiritual without being religious. The value and richness of the spiritual experience is linked to spirituality; not joining a religious group.

In the early phase of a spiritual quest, it is useful to find an image for the spiritual element: Spirit, God, Universal Consciousness, etc. As humans, we struggle with the concept "All is One".

Eastern philosophers and religious leaders tend to give a non-personal identity to the spiritual essence like: "All-encompassing Unknowable", "Universal Principal", etc. and make contact through quiet introspection. The Tao, the Life Force, "Élan vital", Divine Urge, Burning Passion, Infinite Intelligence, Universal Presence are various names which have been given to spiritual energy at different times by diverse cultures.

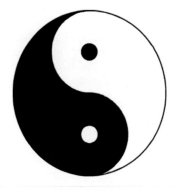

The Judeo-Christian religions have created a human-like divinity, a Supreme Being outside of self, totally exteriorized.

Ones relationship with the Divine will be determined according to the nature and the localization of that spiritual energy in ones perception. People who put God outside of themselves usually relate by asking, pleading, begging, bargaining and imploring (*supplicative* prayer). Christians, for example, ask God to hear and fulfill their prayers.

Those who place spiritual essence within, tend to tap into it directly by affirming their unity with the source (*affirmative* prayer). Those who practice meditation contact the spiritual essence and address it as life, believe it is a source of endless supply and feel part of it.

The loving nature of Divine Essence is another divergent aspect among spiritual and religious people. If God is thought of as being distant (up in the sky), and vengeful (keeping score), then ones relationship with God is highlighted with dread and fear of punishment. If, on the other hand, the Divine is a loving supportive presence providing guidance and creative inspiration, then ones experience of the Divine is of trust and complicity.

Everyone has the ability to change their image of the divine, independent of ones age or cultural background. If an inherited concept of God is not life supporting, one has the option of reassessing ones definition and making sure it conforms to ones present values, beliefs, aspirations and the fundamental right "to pursue happiness".

"The dice of God are loaded in your favor"

Applications of Heart-Smiling to Personal Energy Management

A spiritual relationship that empowers and makes one feel loved and supported is highly recommend. Ones life will be colored by this relationship. The more intimate, intelligent, loving and eternal ones relationship is to a Divine presence, the less apt one is to fall into a victim positioning at some point in life. *To feel alive, we must feel Life within.*

Energy deficiency at the spiritual level is an error in perception, the perception that one is separate from the Source. Spiritual energy is transcendent and integrates us in the vertical dimension, which allows us to experience unity. If one is to feel loved and supported by Universal Power, one must allow for personal divinity through unity.

> **THE SECRET TO BALANCED SPIRITUAL ENERGY IS KNOW THAT LOVE IS THE INDWELLING PRESENCE.**
> **WITH LOVE EVERYTHING IS POSSIBLE.**

"Love is the most universal, most powerful and most mysterious of all cosmic energies"
Pierre Teilhard de Chardin

VI- Inspirational Leadership Energy

> *"What does it mean to be promoted to a leadership position? Frankly. It means to have the authority to serve people in a special way."*
> — Anonymous

Anyone has the option to become the leader of his own life and to inspire others by example. Leaders are driven by personal values such as courage, pride, integrity and compassion and become a source of inspiration to all. Leaders teach by example, by "walking their talk". They inspire those they come in contact with and, consciously or not, become role models.

Having strong values is very energizing. Personal values "move" people. Great spiritual leaders, like Martin Luther King or Gandhi, inspired us, moved us and touched our hearts because of the values they passed on to us. The success of great leaders comes from their ability to mirror back values that inspire and bring out the best in the people they touch.

Leadership is courage in action; courage to follow a calling, to fulfill a mission, and to show vulnerability in the process. Leaders are looked up to and their behavior is often scrutinized. If they fail to live up flawlessly to their claims, they risk blame and shame. The courage to accept vulnerability and imperfection is the mark of a great leader. Values are ideals that can never be perfectly externalized. It takes courage to be willing to try something and, later, to confront shortcomings in the face of failure or setback.

> *"Courage is not the absence of fear; rather, it is judging that something is greater than your fear.*
> — Ambrose Redmoon

Applications of Heart-Smiling to Personal Energy Management

Personal Leadership is a work in progress. With years, our needs and priorities change and values need to be reassessed. What matters when one is 25 years old is not necessarily what is most important at 65. Life cycles force us to evaluate our priorities and driving values constantly. Our society would benefit from a tradition of yearly introspective re-assessment.

HEART-SMILING: IDENTIFY YOUR DRIVING VALUES

1. Bring your attention to your heart and breathe effortlessly from the center of your chest. Become aware of your thoughts, feelings and sensations. Take a moment to identify what matters in your life. Review the driving values in your personal and professional life.

2. Focus again on breathing from the heart. Bring to your consciousness the memory a person that inspired you, or a situation where you experienced the **courage to stand up for** what is important to you and your family. Experience those higher emotions again, right now, and surrender to the warm pleasant feeling this exercise generates. Let a **smile** come to your lips.

3. Pay attention to the changes that are taking place in your body, your attitude and your perception. **Ask your heart** for guidance. Allow what matters most to surface and your driving values to become clear. Identify the 3 most important values and post them as a daily reminder of what you live for. Let these values guide your decisions in all your affairs from now on.

VII- Serving a Higher Purpose Energy

The urge to give back, to make a difference and to leave a spiritual heritage, are examples of living from the level of Energy of Serving a Higher Purpose. Love is perpetually giving of itself and, when we allow Love to operate through us, we embody this urge to give.

Once our basic needs are met, giving comes naturally and we discover the pleasure of giving and sharing with those in need to the point where not giving becomes painful.

Energy circulates and the cycle of receiving and giving back is an illustration of this law. People who have been loved can love in return. Talented people want to share their talents in creative expression. Financially fortunate people enjoy donating to worthy causes. All this feels natural.

Fear of lacking something we need is the only block to the circulation of energy; and ironically, fear of lack is precisely what prevents abundance. This phenomenon is expressed in the well-known phrase: *"There is nothing to fear but fear itself"*. Feeling prosperous attracts abundance and giving becomes satisfying and fulfilling.

Humans also feel the need to pass on the best of what was acquired in ones lifetime onto future generations, be it material conditions, knowledge or pearls of wisdom. One hopes that what was learned and accumulated in ones lifetime will serve to help ones children and future generations.

Applications of Heart-Smiling to Personal Energy Management

HEART-SMILING: SERVING A HIGHER PURPOSE

1. Bring your attention to your heart and breathe effortlessly from the center of your chest. Become aware of your thoughts, feelings and sensations. Identify any discomfort. Contact your natural urge to help those you love.

2. Focus again on breathing from the heart. Bring to your consciousness the memory a person or a situation that made your heart "sing", a situation where you experienced the joy of giving. Experience this emotion again, right now, and surrender to the warm pleasant feeling this exercise generates. Let a **smile** come to your lips

3. Pay attention to the changes taking place in your body, your attitude and your perception. **Ask your heart** to be freed from the fear of lack. Ask your heart to show you examples of service to your family and community. Decide to follow through on these suggestions in order to contribute and make a difference.

As seen earlier, the energy of mastery and transcendence gives one a vertical dimension, connecting one to the higher self. The energy of service connects one to the horizontal dimension. One embraces the human condition and learns to support the Universe by supporting others, by reaching out to other human beings, serving within the community and fostering a loving environment conducive to the blossoming of those we touch.

In conclusion, the Heart-Smiling techniques described above are a few of the applications one can use to manage personal energy. In these seven levels, the pivotal point is level 4 "Operating from the Heart". This central level is the gateway to the energies of mastery and personal leadership.

Heart-Smiling helps one operate from the Heart and is key to integrating all other energy levels. The transformational power of Heart-Smiling will alter ones life and experience of that life in the physical, emotional, mental and spiritual planes. To improve the quality of ones energy (any type of energy) one is invited to use Heart-Smiling and let the Heart show the way to abundant and fulfilling personal energy.

Applications of Heart-Smiling to Personal Energy Management

Chapter 7

What is Energy?

At the beginning of this book, we discussed the principles of personal energy management and presented the seven levels of personal energy. We mentioned that these different forms of energy are intertwined and that "*All is energy*".

Later, we introduced Heart-Smiling, an energy-based technique, which harnesses the powerful energies generated by a state of cardiac coherence and makes them available for our personal use. Since this book addresses personal energy management, let us now consider the nature of energy.

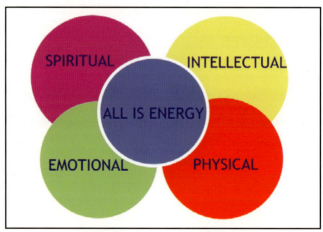

Figure 35: *Interrelation between the different types of energy*

What is Energy?

The Nature of Energy

Energy is a natural force, often synonymous with power. Physicists define energy as a force that can produce work. Kinetic energy, for example, makes objects move in space. Other types of energy are electric, chemical, nuclear, gravitational, etc. One of the fundamental principles in physics confirms that during a reaction, no matter what form it takes, the total amount of energy stays the same.

Einstein's famous equation $E=mc^2$ describes the relation between matter and energy. The material world and the non-material world of energy are interrelated; matter can produce energy and inversely. One of the applications of this law of mass-energy transformation was the creation of the atomic bomb.

The subatomic nature of the world, as described by modern physicists, is very difficult to grasp. Niels Bohr wrote: "Anyone who is not shocked by quantum theory has not understood it."

The continuous exchange between energy and matter at the subatomic level is difficult to imagine because direct observation is impossible. Even more difficult to accept is the notion that observing a reaction affects it, implying that objectivity is a myth in elementary levels.

Applications of Heart-Smiling to Personal Energy Management

What is Reality?

Reality described at that subatomic level seems to be at odds with macroscopic reality. We have been conditioned during our childhood to see reality in a certain way. In his book "Ageless Body, Timeless Mind"[38], Deepak Chopra names this enculturation phenomenon *"the hypnotic state of our collective conditioning."*

We have been conditioned by the society in which we grew up to perceive reality according to norms accepted by the majority. In the time of Galileo, for example, majority perception was that the universe gravitated around the earth. Before Columbus, according to majority perception, reality was that the earth was flat. Reality changes as the majority accepts new discoveries. What is considered a miracle at one era becomes scientific fact in the next.

There is usually a 150-year delay between a scientific discovery and its general acceptance. Discoveries made by quantum physicists at the beginning of the twentieth century, including the theory of relativity, will not be endorsed by our culture for another 50 years.

Only then will "reality" include concepts like Heisenberg's principle of incertitude, based on statistics and not on direct observation; and the principle of subjectivity (not objectivity), which stipulates that observing an experience influences the outcome. The sacrosanct "objective reality" still venerated today is outdated; it is slowly crumbling under the emergence of a new quantum subjective reality.

The Universe and Beyond

Subatomic physicists (studying the "very small") and astrophysicists (studying the "very large") are the new modern explorers. They push forward the frontiers of the unknown by describing a world that we, lay people, cannot even imagine. Cosmology, the science researching the creation of the universe, is fascinating because of the questions it raises. Carl Sagan, Stephen Hawking and Hubert Reeves have followed the evolution of cosmologic discoveries and tryied to find answers to questions that have puzzled human beings since the beginning of time: How did the universe begin? What is the future of the universe? How did the universe evolve from an element as simple as the hydrogen atom to such a huge and complex system inhabited by self-aware conscious beings?

The familiar concepts of time and space are at the core of this exploration. The "Big Bang" theory suggests that the universe was born suddenly and that time, space and matter/anti-matter were created in a sudden flash. "Before" the Big Bang (an oxymoron because the notion of time begins with the Big Bang) was "Singularity", a state not anterior but *beyond* the created universe.

Singularity is a *"pre"*-creation state where temperature, density and energy are infinite; it is an infinite state of oneness that our human brain could never comprehend. In this state, entropy is infinitely negative, which means that disorder is maximum, chaos reigns and creative potential is infinite. Singularity is out of time and space; therefore, it is eternal, always in the present moment, omnipresent and in a state of oneness.

Applications of Heart-Smiling to Personal Energy Management

The words we use to describe singularity like: infinite, eternal, omnipresent, unknowable, and unlimited creative potential, are attributes that traditionally have been the hallmark of spiritual terminology. These terms have been used by different religions to describe the deity, the Absolute.

By using a similar terminology, quantum physicists have shed a new light on the relationship between science and spirituality. Paul Davies[39] wrote: *"Modern science is now closer to God than religion is."* The similarity of terms is evident when describing the pre-creation state. Many modern physicists, cosmologists and astronauts are people who developed an interest for metaphysics "what lies beyond". When asked what was the question he most wanted an answer to, Einstein said: *"I want to know how God created this universe."*

In his book "The God Particle", Nobel price physicist Leon Lederman[40] describes the resolute quest of modern physicists to "visualize" the elusive ultimate particle that could support a unified theory of universal laws. This "God Particle" is that missing building block that would explain all phenomenon of this universe.

Consciousness and Quantum Physics

Quantum physics is concerned with the interaction between the physical world and the world "beyond" from which it is created. This cradle of energy/matter or "quantum soup" is described as a field of information, an intelligent field with creative potential. Physicists talk about a "self-creating universe" that emerges from this creative potential. In his book *"The Self-Aware Universe",* Amit Goswami[41] is suggesting that consciousness is that intelligent field and the "stuff" from which the universe is created.

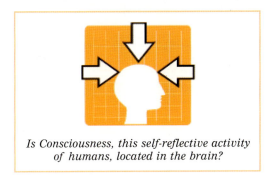

Is Consciousness, this self-reflective activity of humans, located in the brain?

Neuroscientists are also studying consciousness and they define it as the *self-reflective activity* of the brain. Consciousness cannot be located in any structure of the brain; and to track it down neuroscientists are now studying the information-processing centers of the brain. Consciousness seems to be involved with managing information (ideas) and transforming information into chemical energy.

Could it be that this "intelligent field with creative potential" described by physicists is the same as the "information-processing consciousness" that neurologists are hunting down?

Consciousness and Reality

Consciousness, the ability to have an inner experience, is something everyone possesses. However, the manner in which each individual experiences consciousness is unique and determines ones personal reality.

One has the illusion that one is experiencing directly the reality of the physical world. Unfortunately, this is a perception error: the colors, sounds, textures and odors we perceive are not 'out there'; these sensations are constructs of our brain.

When a photon hits our retina, it releases energy, which is transformed into visual images. We do not see light directly, we experience it through the energy it releases. The sequence of neurochemical events that take place after a photon hits our retina is determined by our programming and is immediately translated into an experience of reality that is constructed in the mind.

Peter Russell, a Cambridge physicist, uses the analogy of light from a movie projector to describe consciousness. The projector sends light to the screen. This light is modified and images are produced.

The images we are conscious of are the perceptions and sensations we experience. They are the content of the experience. In a movie, they would be the story. According to Russell's analogy, light, without which no image is possible, corresponds to the faculty of consciousness.

What is Energy?

We all know that the images on the screen are made of light, but we usually do not pay attention to the light itself, we focus on the images and the stories they tell. We experience the movie, not the light. With the age of digitalization, the analogy is even stronger because the images are formed according to bits of information; and consciousness then becomes analogous to a virtual entity, a field that holds the information data. In this analogy, the data processor is the brain.

With the advent of quantum physics, our concept of the building blocks of matter went from small spheres organized like mini solar systems, to fuzzy clouds of probabilities with no definite speed or location. At this subatomic level the physical world is inaccessible to our senses. Worse, it is unknowable because the very fact of observing it makes it collapse into a limited form that does not reflect its totality.

Light is a non-material entity that exists outside of time. Photons, subatomic particles carrying light, have interesting characteristics. Photons have no mass (they are not material) and they can travel through the entire universe without losing energy. According to the relativity theory, time ceases to exist at the speed of light. For the photon, time does not exist.

Light is a non-material entity that connects the entire universe. Any exchange of energy between atoms involves an exchange of photons, therefore, all interactions in the material world are mediated by light.

Applications of Heart-Smiling to Personal Energy Management

In his book "From Science to God" Peter Russell[42] evokes the possibility that light, the non-material connector of the cosmos, is also the "stuff" consciousness is made of, that which gives us inner experience. His hypothesis is based on the similarities that both light and consciousness share. They are both non-material and outside of time. Even though they are universal, they can only be experienced at the individual level. It is impossible to 'see' light directly. We can only experience images through the construct of our brain. In a similar manner, universal consciousness is impossible to grasp, each individual use of it becomes a unique life experience.

What's more, it is also not possible to observe an external objective reality. Reality is always personal and subjective because our individual brains filter sensorial input. Even if there were an objective reality out there, independent of observation, our filtering brains impede us from knowing it.

***Reality as we experience it is ALWAYS an interpretation;
it is the reality our brain makes known to us.***

Each person perceives reality according to their brain filter.

144

The Illusion of Separation

Mystics of all traditions have described the transcendental experience of oneness with a "Universal Being". Through a non-ordinary state of consciousness, mystics access a dimension out of time and space where they experience the bliss of oneness. When they return, they can't seem to find the words to tell about their experience, but they are unanimous to affirm that there exists another way of being, a way where the individual merges with the universal, and that separation is an illusion.

To try to grasp the concept of 'one-becoming-many', let us use the analogy of light dispersed by a prism. Let's substitute light for consciousness and try to understand how separation is an illusion. When white light goes through a prism, it is dispersed into many monochromatic rays of rainbow colors. Let's imagine a green ray of dispersed light. If I am that green ray, it is hard to imagine that my green-self shares source and identity with a blue other. Because the human brain is not able to access the concept of "universal" directly, we are constrained to our individual interpretation.

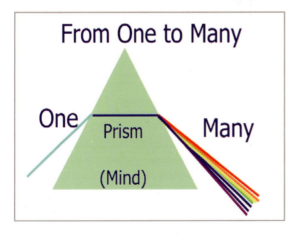

Figure 36: Dispersion of light. When white light goes through a prism, it is dispersed in many monochrome rays.

Applications of Heart-Smiling to Personal Energy Management

The fact that we perceive each other as separate is an illusion created by reality passing through the brain (prism). Individual consciousness, experienced through the filtering brain does not allow one to perceive oneness with other individual consciousness (colored lights) nor with universal consciousness (white light).

Universal consciousness experiences plurality through the prism of individual minds creating the illusion of separation. The "bliss of oneness" is experienced only beyond the veil of illusion.

When studying the energies involved in practicing the Heart-Smiling technique, it is important to highlight that the *Heart is the interface between the Universal and the individual.* It is in the heart that resides the capacity for transcendence. The individual self connects with Universal Self at level of the Heart and experiences divine oneness.

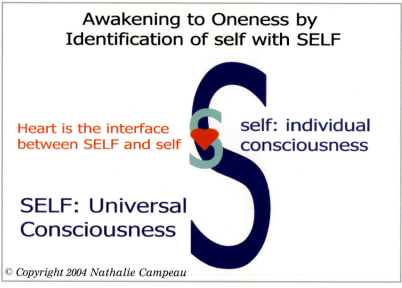

Figure 37: *Identification of individual consciousness with Universal Consciousness is the key to awakening from the hypnotic state created by our brains. Heart, the interface between universal and individual, is the gateway to this unifying state of consciousness.*

What is Energy?

These fleeting moments of mystical experiences are so powerful that people who live them usually dedicate their lives in pursuit of their meaning. The meaning often takes the form of a calling that cannot be denied.

There is opportunity to experience this transcendent connection at each energy level. At the physical level, athletes experience "the zone" where pain and tiredness disappear and the silent rhythm of ones heart and the Universe are one. At the sexual level, orgasm creates a "fusion of souls", whereas, at the emotional level, the warm comforting feeling of bonded oneness applies to the love between family members or group members. At the intellectual level, it is the Eureka experience of discovery and understanding; while the ease, grace, focus and flow felt at achievement belong to the level of mastery. At the level of service, it is the great joy and satisfaction of being useful and making a difference.

Fusion of the souls moments create a mystical experience.

147

Applications of Heart-Smiling to Personal Energy Management

Transcendence is at the origin of great accomplishments, record breaking, long-term commitments, decisions to have children, important discoveries, and the decision to "follow ones bliss" and passionately carry out a mission on purpose.

The Heart connection, experienced in a human love relationship is, in fact, the connection to Universal Love through the loved one. Universal Love can only experience love through individuals. *"God needs man"*. Universal Love needs an outlet, a subject/object to love. Man was created as that outlet, someone to love. The whole creation is an act of love.

"Love loves to love". Universal Love experiences a myriad of possible love experiences through the human love experience. In this sense, by creating "otherness" Universal Love experiences manifestations of love. The energies the love experience creates circulate in the act of giving and receiving love. The purpose of human existence is an outlet for the energies of Love.

Humans are created to be "loving devices" through which the energies of Universal Love flow. Each time one loves; the mission is fulfilled. Each time one loves, one experiences Universal Love and Universal Love is nourished and grows. Through the experience of love one becomes a love-channel for Universal Love to love.

Humans are "loving devices"

When one falls in love, one has the impression the other is bringing to the relationship something that was not there before. We feel more complete and whole (the "soul mate" syndrome). This, however, is a perceptual error. As a manifestation of Universal Love, everyone is already whole and complete.

Separation is always an illusion. All humans are distinct forms of the same essence, diffractions of the Universal Love source. The ecstasy of fusion one experiences in a love union is the human experience closest to the human race's real nature, that of "Beings of Love".

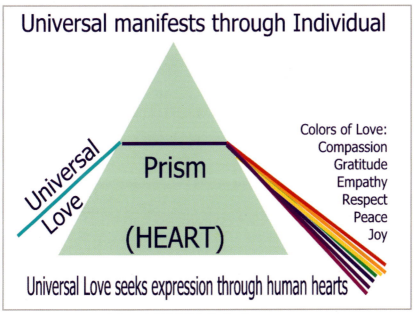

© Copyright 2004 Nathalie Campeau

Figure 38: *Universal manifests through individual. Universal Love is channeled through individual hearts to express its "colors", which are compassion, gratitude, empathy, respect, joy and peace. Practicing Heart-Smiling, is allowing Universal Love to operate through our individual hearts.*

Applications of Heart-Smiling to Personal Energy Management

"A human being is a part of the whole, called by us 'Universe," a part limited in time and space. He experiences himself, his thoughts and feelings as something separated from the rest -- a kind of optical delusion of consciousness. This delusion is a kind of prison for us, restricting us to our personal desires and to affection for a few persons nearest to us. Our task must be to free ourselves from this prison by widening our circle of compassion to embrace all living creatures and the whole of nature in its beauty."
— Albert Einstein

During the practice of the Heart-Smiling technique, which uses the Heart as a gateway to Universal Self, one experiences transcendence. Individual Heart *is* the Universal Heart. The experience of Oneness, like the experience of love, takes place in the Heart. Practicing Heart-Smiling allows Universal Heart to channel the individual heart.

Heart –Smiling is a method that puts one in contact with Source. It awakens one to a non-separate way of being and allows the individual to taste the bliss of oneness. By practicing Heart-Smiling we channel Universal Love through our individual hearts and allow Love to show its "colors": compassion, gratitude, empathy, respect, joy and peace.

The relationship between Universal and individual is one of co-creation. An individual creates his/her own experience by tapping into the unlimited universal creative power and channeling it through the individual mind.

Quantum physics teaches us that an observer is necessary to collapse a wave of probability into a material particle. In a similar manner, individual consciousness is needed to materialize (bring into the material world) our personal experiences from the universal field of potentiality.

Our only limits are those we accept for ourselves. Our cage opens from the inside. The cage itself is only an illusion.

Energy/Matter Exchanges at the Cellular Level

As seen earlier, the exchange of energy and matter at the cellular level, is interchangeable. Electrons, photons and other particles are constantly being exchanged. These particles of matter emerge from the "quantum soup", and this constant exchange of energy and particles is the background work for atom and molecule formation. Each one of our cells is continually remodeling thanks to a constant flow of carbon, oxygen, nitrogen, calcium, sodium, etc. As a result, each year we renew 98% of our atom content.

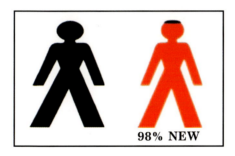

Our bodies are Constantly Transforming

Our cells die at varying rates depending on how specialized there are. The inner layer of our intestines is replaced every few days. Our skin is renewed every five weeks, and even our bones that we like to think of as strong and stable are rebuilt every three months.

If we renew our cellular material all the time, how do we stay the same? The answer is programming. We are doubly programmed. First, our genetic programming, embedded in the chromosomes of each of our cells, creates and oversees all cell function. Our cellular memory, another type of programming, recognizes past intruders like viruses and greets them anew with resisting antibodies. Cellular memory also maintains traumatic scars despite the process of skin renewal.

Healing Principles

The body is intelligent. It knows at every moment what it needs to function optimally and how to auto-regulate internal balance, a function known as homeostasis. It has a built-in healing capacity. Damaged organs know how to self-repair and the body benefits from renewed materials flowing in all the time.

This innate wisdom can be tapped into to heal and maintain the body in a perfectly healthy state. One can also assist ones body and harness this self-healing capacity by listening and deciphering signals it constantly sends. It is very useful to learn to read these signals and to become aware of our internal climate.

To enjoy radiant health, perfect balance and optimal functioning, we rely on cellular intelligence and natural cycles. Nature proceeds in cycles: birth, growth, maturation, destruction and death. New cells are made, they mature, they function at full potential, they die and they are replaced. The human body also has its cycles: time to grow; time to be fully active; time to rest and regenerate. Awareness of these cycles allows us to assist bodily function, help it be completely operational and maintain its balance.

Because energy and matter are interrelated, working on energy can help transform the body. Learning to manage energy is essential to restoring and maintaining splendid health. This is the object of the next chapter entitled "Discover your Energy Type".

What is Energy?

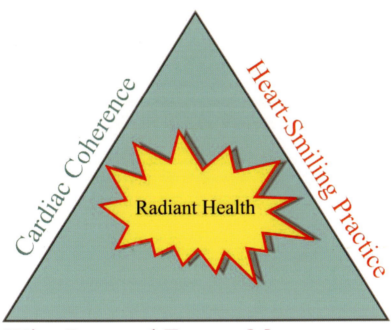

Applications of Heart-Smiling to Personal Energy Management

Chapter 8

Discover your Energy Type

Heart-Smiling, a cardiac coherence-inducing technique, synergizes brain-heart energies, balances internal chemistry and harmonizes organ function. The brain is a major player in the formation of hormones that influence inner chemistry balance. This chapter will help understand how bran chemistry can unconsciously affect personal energy, attitudes and many of our day-to-day decisions. The way we treat the information delivered by our senses and our internal monitors is based on the type of chemical our brain produces. This chapter describes those chemicals and explains their affiliation with types of energy.

Hormones, like insulin or cortisol, facilitate chemical reactions and play a central role in energy production. The hypothalamus and pituitary glands in the brain control most bodily hormone function. Neurons are specialized brain cells that produce hormones called neurotransmitters, whose role is to relay information from one neuron to the next.

Neurons

The human brain contains about a hundred billion neurons, each one having up to one hundred thousand connections with other neurons. Every second, billions of transmissions are accomplished through liberation of chemical messengers called *neurotransmitters* in response to electrical stimulation of the cell membrane. Neurotransmitters are synthesized and stored in the neuron and are liberated in the synaptic junction, a gap between any two cells.

Once in the synaptic junction, neurotransmitters bind with the specific receptors on the membrane of next neuron (postsynaptic). Membrane receptors have an exact complementary three-dimensional structure, which allows them to recognize and "capture" their specific neurotransmitters. Dopamine for example, can only be captured by dopaminergic receptors. Once the receptors are engaged with dopamine molecules, they signal the nucleus of the receiving neuron that information has been transmitted.

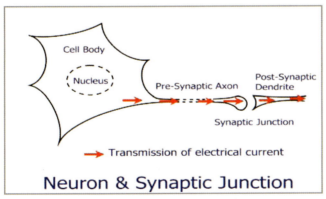

Figure 39: *Electrical current spreads from the axon of the sending cell to the dendrite of the receiving cell by depolarization of the cellular membrane, which liberates neurotransmitters in the synaptic junction (gap between the neurons).*

Applications of Heart-Smiling to Personal Energy Management

The sequence of this neurotransmission is illustrated in figure 40:

1. Neurotransmitters are synthesized from precursor amino acids in the body of the neuron sending the message.

2. Neurotransmitters are stored in synaptic vesicles at the end of the axon. An electrical signal, which depolarizes the neuron's cell membrane, will trigger the vesicles to release their content.

3. Neurotransmitters are liberated into the synaptic gap.

4. Neurotransmitters are captured by specific receptors on the cell membrane of the receiving neuron where structural changes notify the receiving neuron.

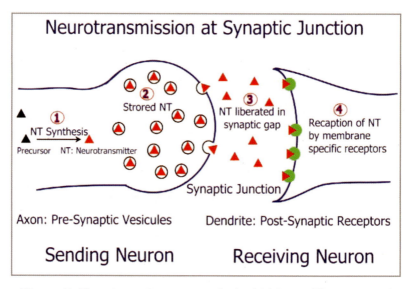

Figure 40: *Neurotransmitters are synthesized (1) by specific neurons using precursor amino acid. They are then stored (2) in synaptic vesicles. An electrical signal (depolarization) will trigger their content release into the synaptic gap or junction (3). Once in the gap they are captured (4) by specific receptors on the membrane of the receiving neuron. Structural changes on the membrane notify the receiving neuron.*

Information transmission from one cell to the next is a complex event involving electrical, chemical and structural changes. The efficacy of the transmission is assured by the tri-dimensional and biochemical affinities specific to each neurotransmitter.

Synthesis of Neurotransmitters

There are many Neurotransmitters. The most well known are Adrenaline, Dopamine, Serotonin and Endorphins. Each one is built from a specific amino acid. Dopamine is made from phenylalanine and serotonin from tryptophane. Adrenaline and noradrenaline are also synthesized from phenylalanine, the former in the adrenal glands and the latter in the brain.

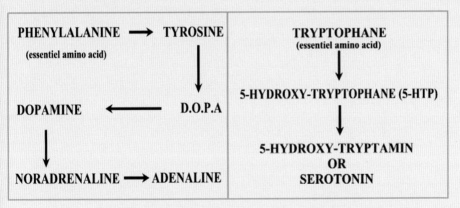

Figure 41: Synthesis of dopamine and adrenaline from phenylalanine. Synthesis of serotonin from tryptophane

The brain uses neurotransmitters to internalize information from our environment and create emotion, sensation and perception. When seeing a spider, for example, is interpreted as a sign of danger, it triggers the secretion of neurotransmitters in our brain, which produce the experience of fear.

Applications of Heart-Smiling to Personal Energy Management

A physical sensation can be associated with more than one emotion. A roller coaster ride, for example, may increase the secretion of heart-accelerating adrenaline, which may produce the sensation of excitement and fun in some, while creating a horrible nightmare for others.

Specific Neurotransmitters Induce Specific Behaviors

Behavior is determined by the predominance of neurotransmitters in ones system. Each neurotransmitter fosters specific behavior according to its stimulating or inhibiting abilities.

> **1. Dopamine Stimulates.** A dopamine-driven personality tends to be impulsive, excitable, enjoys exploring, takes risks, gets bored easily, and seeks novelty. They are often accused of instability because, as soon as routine sets in, they get bored and make changes in their lives.
>
> They are thrill seekers and enjoy activities like car racing and skydiving. If divers, they will not be satisfied with snorkeling and observing the colorful fish at the surface; they will want to become scuba divers and explore wrecks at abysmal depths. This personality would be very unhappy in a clerical position.

Discover your Energy Type

2. Serotonin Inhibits. Serotonin-driven persons tend to maintain the status quo; they do not want to rock the boat, and try to avoid conflicts and problems at any cost. They enjoy taking care of others and protecting the weak. They are very sensitive to rejection and prefer to endure an abusive situation rather than fight.

Serotonin-driven persons make dedicated helping professionals or teachers but they are not attracted to sales. Serotonin deficiency has been identified in people who suffer from many types of depression. Many new antidepressants increase Serotonin levels in the brain.

3. Adrenaline/Noradrenaline Maintains. Adrenaline is at the core of the fight or flight reaction and other conditioned responses. Adrenaline-driven personalities will repeat behaviors that are rewarding and are often productive, hard working, ambitious and successful.

They are the 'Type A' personalities described in scientific literature, the overachievers and workaholics that literally open themselves to all sorts of stress related diseases, including premature heart attacks. They make good business leaders, high-level managers and sales directors and usually are not happy in a position where no advancement is foreseeable.

Neurotransmitters and Personality types

Heredity plays an important role in our personality type because our brain chemistry, which is to a great extent influenced by our genetic code, predisposes us to adopt certain behaviors rather than others.

We are born with a genetic tendency to produce more of a certain type of neurotransmitter, and because each neurotransmitter is associated with specific behavioral patterns, it is possible to link personality types with neurotransmitters.

The following diagram illustrates the association of three neurotransmitters: adrenaline, dopamine and serotonin with personality types classified respectively as the **Builder**, the **Explorer,** and the **Protector**.

© Copyright 2005 Nathalie Campeau

Figure 42: *The Builder is associated with Adrenaline, the Explorer with Dopamine and the Protector with Serotonin.*

Discover your Energy Type

Identify your Preferred Neurotransmitter

Because we are constantly under the influence of our neurotransmitters, it is very helpful to learn to read their signals. By taking time out and doing quiet introspection, one can easily train oneself to recognize which neurotransmitter is controlling the mindscape at any given time. Here are a few guidelines to help you identify them:

- When **Dopamine** is prevalent, novelty seeking, risk taking, and boredom avoidance are key issues.

- **Adrenaline** is involved with performance, being the best, and the need for approval. It triggers competitiveness, persistence and tenacity.

- **Serotonin** is involved with feeling satiated, useful and peaceful.

Each of us has a preferred neurotransmitter, one that dominates the picture in certain circumstances. The dominant neurotransmitter is always modulated by secondary neurotransmitters bringing nuances to the situation. One can be genetically inclined to be adrenergic (adrenaline-driven), and choose to be serotonin-driven in certain situations. For example, a successful and competitive businesswoman (adrenaline-driven) can still like to cuddle in a soft blanket at home after work and eat ice cream (a serotonin-driven characteristic).

Identifying which neurotransmitter is 'speaking' at any one moment is a skill that can be acquired. The chart below summarizes different characteristics and typical behaviors associated with each personality type, including behavioral disorders and diseases associated with a deficiency of the influencing neurotransmitter.

Type	Builder	Explorer	Protector
Preferred NT	Adrenaline	Dopamine	Serotonin
Role	Climbs the ladder	Pushes limits	Protects Peace and Maintains Status Quo
Worst Enemy	Fear of not being good enough	Boredom	Troubled Peace
Motto	More!	Far out!	Don't rock the boat!
Shadow Side	Dictator «Shark»	Outcast Lost	Controlling Passive-Aggressive
Disease	Stress Anxiety, Panic	Antisocial Psychotic	Depression Obsessive-Compulsive

© Copyright 2005 Nathalie Campeau

Table 8: *Personality types and their preferred Neurotransmitter (NT)*

People usually identify with more than one of these categories because various neurotransmitters are present in the human system at different levels at any one time.

Discover your Energy Type

The Builder is the personality most favorably acknowledged by industrial societies. This personality is hard working and competition-driven with the qualities of a natural leader and is often in a responsible work position like manager, supervisor or head of department. Very comfortable in a corporate environment, the Builder successfully climbs the ladder driven by ambition and the need for recognition.

This adrenaline-driven personality is susceptible to stress related illnesses like heart attacks, stomach ulcers, panic attacks, burnout and the Japanese Karoshi syndrome (sudden death by overwork). The success-driven Builder neglects family, health, and personal life and is at risk of becoming a workaholic capable of literally killing himself with work. In today's society, builders are praised, taken advantage of and finally disposed of when they cannot keep up with expectations.

Builders live for "more"; more money, more fame, bigger car, bigger house, latest gadgets - everything that's faster, newer and bigger. They often become the "sharks" that eat anything that stands between them and success. This darker side of the Builder comes from the belief that more is better at any cost. They are natural leaders but become dictators and abusers when power-hungry maneuvers are frustrated.

Winston Churchill was a good example of a Builder.

The Explorer is the non-compliant mischievous and eternal child of our society, with little respect for rules and conventions. These novelty seekers are attracted by virgin territory. Very curious and creative, they urge others to open to all the possibilities in any given situation. They inspire others to expand their knowledge and to push themselves to the limit of their comfort zone.

Explorers are free thinkers, philosophers, research scientists, site photographers, frontline journalists, artists and professional detractors.

The down side of the Explorer is his insatiable need for novelty. Many times accused of being irresponsible and unstable, the Explorer can leave projects and people behind when dominated by an inherited craving for newness. Often going too far, becoming marginal, isolated, ostracized, they can feel rejected and misunderstood.

When dopamine production is too impaired, either because of heredity or drug abuse, Explorers can become psychotic and totally lose contact with reality. Psychotics live in a world of their own, seeing things that others do not see or hearing things that others do not hear. Schizophrenia is a genetic dopamine disorder.

Cocaine abusers can deplete their dopamine stock and experience psychotic episodes. During those paranoid crises, they become terrified, hide behind the curtains and spy on the street to see who is "out there to get them". Cocaine addicts can also suffer tactile hallucinations. They feel 'bugs' under their skin and try desperately to get rid of them at any cost. They usually cover their arms with long sleeves to hide the marks of self-inflicted wounds and injection 'tracks'.

The life of an Explorer is not a restful one.

Many Rock Stars are Explorers.

Serotonin-driven Protectors are happy when all is calm! They cherish peace of mind and try to avoid troubles at any cost. They make up the 'silent majority' of industrialized societies and love the routine of every day life. Protectors (worker bees) execute and comply with orders, take extreme pleasure in a job well done, and proudly contribute to the maintenance of law and order.

Protectors will put the common good before their personal needs in order to assure that the status quo be maintained. Protectors like routine tasks (that Builders and Explorers would not touch with a ten-foot pole) and are not inclined to personal initiative.

Protectors are the breeders and homemakers finding great joy and fulfillment in caring for others. A Protector with an empty home becomes easily susceptible to the "Empty Nest Syndrome". Protectors' favorite leisure time activity is 'cocooning' with a book or a movie, cuddling, daydreaming, or even cooking or cleaning the house.

The down side of the Protector comes from the difficulty to deal with change. The Protector motto is "Don't rock the boat". Risk is not welcome. At the workplace, Protectors often resist the implementation of new programs. At home, they have a hard time with the children becoming self-reliant and tend to be overprotective with them.

Because serotonin is involved with satiety (the sensation of having enough to eat and to drink), many eating disorders are caused by serotonin dysfunction. Serotonin enhancers are now the treatment of choice for depression and OCD (Obsessive-Compulsive Disorder), both associated with serotonin deficiency.

Other Important Neurotransmitters

Endorphins have a chemical structure close to that of morphine and are produced by the brain and other organs. When present in the blood, they produce a feeling of well-being, fulfillment, inner peace and satisfaction. They are often referred to as the "pleasure hormones". In a sexual arena, dopamine stimulates action to fulfill needs and produce desire, where as endorphins produce pleasure.

An imbalance in the production of these hormones has been documented in the research literature regarding addiction, as inducing insatiable craving. Desire grows with each drug use, but the chance for pleasure lessens. The gap created between increased desire (dopamine) and not enough pleasure (endorphins) pushes addicts to use over and over.

GABA - Gamma Amino Butyric Acid - is made from the amino acid glutamine. This neurotransmitter has a calming effect on humans because it slows down brain activity. The action mechanism of many drugs, including alcohol and Benzodiazepines (Valium, etc.), involves GABA receptors. GABA is a "downer" and causes one to relax. GABA inducung drugs in high doses can slow down brain function to the point of deep sleep, coma and death by respiratory arrest.

GABA deficiency creates feelings of anxiety, restlessness, exhaustion, and sleep disorders. A typical example of GABA dysfunction is in alcohol withdrawal. Alcoholics will experience anxiety, restlessness, fatigue and difficulty sleeping, 6 to 8 hours after the last drink. By administering a drug from the Benzodiazepine family at that moment, the GABA deficiency will be corrected and withdrawal symptoms will disappear.

Acetylcholine is the neurotransmitter of the parasympathetic system. It is responsible for transmitting along the Vagus nerve between the heart and the base of the brain. Acetylcholine dysfunction leads to vaso-vagal episodes, charactarized a sensation of weakness or even passing out in tense situations like the sight of blood, fathers in delivery rooms, waiting in line too long.

Neurotransmitters and personal programming

Genetic programming and human conditioning determine the predominance of specific neurotransmitters and neurotransmitter-mediated behavioral reactions. Eons of ancestral programming trigger typical reactions. Darkness, thunder, snakes, tigers, and guns elicit fear (adrenaline). Food stimulates hunger (Serotonin). A genuine smile opens the heart (endorphins).

More conditioning is brought into the picture by personal development. Traumatic reaction to dramatic situations in the family of origin is often related to dysfunctional behavior. Fear of abuse in the presence of authority figures, fear of being engulfed in the presence of smothering mother figures, fear of dying when experiencing rejection, shame in the face of failure are all examples of conditional dysfunction.

Individual family programming is embedded deep in our subconscious and shapes our reactions and behaviors in the following manner. Every emotional reaction is mediated by a specific neurotransmitter. Each time a fear or shame-inducing situation reoccurs, a specific neurotransmitter triggers the resurgence of the emotional memory associated with that traumatic event.

Losing at tennis may shame one who was traumatized by shame during the formative years. Likewise, an angry boss may trigger terror in a person who has suffered in the hands of an abusive authority figure.

Man tends to associate values like good / bad or pleasant / unpleasant to experience thereby associating that value with the activated neurotransmitter. In this way, people predetermine the value of an experience. For example, if it is snowing in the morning (a neutral situation, intrinsically neither good nor bad) past experience with snow will dictate a person's reaction. The sight of snow for a skier may announce a delightful day skiing and put him in a good mood. For a person who previously suffered a car accident in the snow, the sight of snow may trigger fear and anxiety.

Sequence of Brain Interpretation:

1) The brain picks up a signal and converts it to energy,

2) Energy is instantaneously translated into neurotransmitters,

3) Neurotransmitters evoke feelings, which, along with past experience, determine present experience.

Neurotransmitters run ones life if allowed to dictate emotional reaction. It is imperative that people learn to reassess perceptions and choose how to experience an event.

Event—> Programming —>Perception —> Emotions—> Experience

The human brain is a sophisticated computer and projects a person's perception of reality. This fact creates the inherent illusion that man is 'a victim of circumstance', when, in fact, people choose to experience according to reality based on individual perception.

Changing Perception by Engaging the Heart

In order to escape the conditioned neurotransmitter trap, one needs to change ones programming and suppress the associated sensation-neurotransmitter-perception reflex. In this way, one frees oneself of conditioning and behavioral precedents.

People who learn to engage their hearts before reacting will be able to choose how to experience each situation as it arises. Learning to stop the automatic cerebral input of past experiences will enable one to face each life situation as if it were the first time and see it through new eyes.

Can you imagine that if each time it snowed, people would see it as if it were the first time ever, with the eyes of innocent children? How much more fascinating our lives would be!

> **Event—> New Perception—> Emotions—> New Experience**

Applications of Heart-Smiling to Personal Energy Management

Wisdom and Innocence

Remembering the facts related to an experience and disengaging from emotional content enables man to be innocent and wise at the same time. Human survival depends on past learning, of course. We do not have to reinvent the wheel each time we face a problem. The accumulation and use of past experience enables man to choose more appropriately in the present. Remembering what happened in the past and the consequences but being able to approach a situation with no emotional precedent, opens the door to the option of a new "innocent" experience.

We refuse innocence every time we say *"This is the way I am"*. Famous phrase like *"I am what I am!"* or *"It's always the same, nothing changes under the sun"* or *"life is a perpetual repeating of itself"* are all examples of our refusal to choose freedom. Claudia Black[43] in her book on Children of Alcoholics suggests that, to embrace innocence *"all it takes is a little willingness to see things differently"*.

One who has achieved this integration, one who has become wise and innocent is free and no longer conditioned by past programming. The "Wise-Innocent" will remember the past and learn from it but will not let it dictate present reactions. The Wise-Innocent archetype deserves our attention because persons who embody it can tap into childlike wonder and awe, access mature sensible insights, makes better decisions and consciously become a happier person.

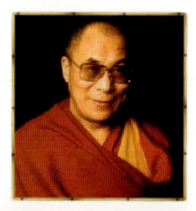

Take Control and Stop Neurotransmitters from Running Your Life

The brain is the grandest of illusionists. It filters sensorial signals through perception, interpretation and memory, and transforms the results into a personal experience. Eyes, for example, inform the brain they have detected a face. In less than a second, the brain transforms this information into the joy of meeting a friend or the alerting fear of a threatening encounter.

The brain speaks so quickly and eloquently that one experiences reality as something that exists outside oneself when, in fact, reality only exists exactly as we know it in our brains. As seen before, both perception and consciousness are deeply personal and subjective and occur internally.

A complex chain of events (not yet completely understood by researchers) occurs between the time a signal is gathered by ones senses and the moment one experiences. In the last few decades many discoveries in the field of neuroscience have helped us better understand many structural and functional aspects of the brain, including the role of neurotransmitters.

Psychiatrists and Addiction Medicine professionals have benefited greatly from these findings. Addiction is one of the best examples of the hostile take over and consequent entrapment of a person by disturbed brain chemistry caused by neurotransmitter imbalance.

Addictions are an example of a hostile take over of a person by disturbed brain chemistry.

Applications of Heart-Smiling to Personal Energy Management

Addictions lie. They make promises they do not keep. They deceive addicts with the mirage of artificial paradise. Addicts are tricked by their neurotransmitters. Addiction, by definition, is the tendency to continue using the addicting substance or performing compulsive behavior despite negative consequences.

Neurotransmitters rule when an addict continues to use his drug despite the negative consequences of losing his health, his job, his family, his life. Neurotransmitters rule when alcoholics continue drinking after being diagnosed with liver problems or a stomach ulcer. Neurotransmitters rule when cocaine addicts keep using despite the financial predicaments. These insane behaviors are, without a doubt, caused by neurotransmitter imbalance.

Judgment and Denial

Judgment is one of the higher functions of the forebrain related to normal neurochemical performance. The incapacity to connect substance use to harmful consequence is called denial, one of addiction's major symptoms. Denial is a form of impaired judgment and a result of neurotoxicity caused by psychoactive drugs.

An addict's judgment is impaired. They mistake consequence for cause. Alcoholic patients, for example, do not see that their spouse is leaving because of the drinking, instead they think the reverse. They drink because their spouse does not understand them or expected too much.

My wife has become a monter... if you had my wife, you would drink too.

Popular denial phrases are: *"If you had my spouse, you'd drink, too!" "I drink because of him/her!" "My boss is always on my case, I need those drink/pills/drugs to put up with him."*

When, during treatment, chemical balance is restored in the brain, denial goes away.

Gambling, eating disorders, compulsive shopping and compulsive sexual disorders are other forms of addiction. These self-destructive compulsive behaviors are also the result of neurotransmitter imbalance. Addicts' brain does not function normally. Judgment, affect and decision-making are impaired.

The most effective treatment of addiction involves correcting brain chemistry and neurotransmitter rebalancing. Dopamine resources are completely depleted in cocaine addicts and their withdrawal symptoms reflect this. Cocaine addicts in withdrawal lose their drive, become fatigued, apathetic, bored and don't find pleasure in any thing. During acute and sub-acute stages of withdrawal, which may last many weeks, an addict's normal neurotransmitter production must be restored in order to minimize the risk of relapse.

The Addiction Trap

When one uses alcohol or drugs the first time and feels good afterwards, this behavior usually gets repeated. With each additional use, however, the pleasurable effects diminish and dysphoria (feeling bad) eventually sets in. To make things even worse, shame enters the picture when one realizes how irresponsible one is behaving. If the person is predisposed to addiction, there is only one way to feel better: use again!

Applications of Heart-Smiling to Personal Energy Management

This is how the addiction cycle begins:
- ☹ One uses a substance (or repeat a behavior) to feel better.
- ☹ The effects wear off.
- ☹ The substance or behavior is repeated in order to stop feeling bad.

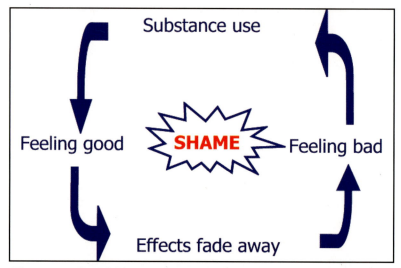

Figure 43: The Addiction Trap with shame core: Using a substance to feel good, and when the effects wear out, the need to use again in order to stop feeling bad.

An addict, by definition is one who has lost control over substance use and is controlled by the addiction. An addict knows at some point that he should cut down, but cannot. At the core of every addiction, there is a *deep sense of helplessness, worthlessness and shame*. The outcome is always loss: loss of self-esteem and ability to enjoy life.

Addicts suffer severely in the areas of:
- Brain chemistry imbalance
- Behavior control
- Self-esteem
- Ability to enjoy life

All these factors are somehow related to impaired neurotransmitters.

Personality Types and Drug of Choice

With years of experience in the addiction field, I noticed some degree of association between personality types and their drug of choice:
- The **Builder (Adrenaline)**: alcohol
- The **Explorer (Dopamine)**: cocaine
- The **Protector (Serotonin)**: opiates (heroine and narcotics) and Benzodiazepines (drugs in the Valium family)

There are many exceptions to this classification, and most addicts are multiple-substance abusers. For example, "speed ball" (very popular with Explorers) is a mixture of cocaine and heroin in the same syringe used to enhance the high and reduce the "crash" phase.

Builders will mix alcohol and cocaine in order to drink more without feeling their judgment is impaired. Builders easily develop a cross addiction with sleeping pills and other drugs doctors prescribe to help them calm down.

Heroin addicts often use marijuana when heroin is not available. Today, multiple dependencies are more the rule than the exception. Treatment recommendations always include abstinence from all addictive psychoactive drugs in order to avoid cross addictions. No matter the drug of choice, the addict in treatment is required to be substance free: no alcohol, no drugs, and no addictive medication.

Nicotine addiction is still very prevalent and equally distributed among the three types of personalities. Cigarettes contain nicotine and dozens of other toxic substances, many of which are carcinogenic. Cigarettes are strongly addictive because they blend stimulants and relaxants, thereby making one more alert and calmer at the same time.

Smokers self-administer this drug by inhalation (similar to crack) every 20 to 60 minutes to keep their blood levels stable and to avoid the withdrawal symptoms of anxiety, difficulty concentrating, irritability, cravings, etc. Smokers use many drugs at the same time.

Addiction is a severe problem; it robs one of family, freedom of choice and a life of quality, among other things. Trust, respect, freedom and safety are all excluded from the addict's reality as long as addiction is present. To break the cycle of addiction, treatment is needed. Abstinence is not the goal of treatment but is the pre-requisite to recovery. Medical supervision of withdrawal helps restore normal brain chemistry. In order for recovery to be a complete success, professionals must address second-phase issues like shame and self-esteem.

Part of an effective relapse prevention program should identify valid substitutes for the effects of the substance being abandoned. For example, if someone is using a drug to cope with shyness or stress, it is important to teach the addict other strategies to deal with these issues. As mentioned earlier, boredom is the number one enemy of the dopamine-driven Explorer. Relapse prevention, then, must include balancing dopamine levels and training patients to deal with boredom.

Alcohol Anonymous' 12-steps program is based on a spiritual process. This effective group program has been adapted for many different kinds of situations dealing with addictive personality disorders. Lives, according to the 12-steps program must be turned over to a greater power in order to regain self-love and self-respect. The spiritual aspect of the addict's personality is engaged in the recovery process. The 12-step program is the first holistic approach to addiction recovery in Western society.

Discover your Energy Type

Heart-Smiling also offers a spiritual approach. This technique taps into the energies of the heart to harmonize heart-brain chemistry, with the intention of balancing personal energy at all the physical, emotional, mental and spiritual levels. Practicing Heart-Smiling can help those struggling with addiction. This technique has the power to transform the perception addicts have of themselves and give them the strength to modify their behavior by adopting a more loving and respectful self-image. Only the superior transforming energies of the heart have that power to heal this devastating disease.

Heart-Smiling: Self-Love for Addicts & Co-Dependents

1. Bring your attention to your heart and breathe effortlessly from the center of your chest. Become aware of your thoughts, feelings and sensations; scan your body for any discomfort. Identify your energy type and prevalent neurotransmitter. Realize that your neurotransmitters are robbing you of your freedom of choice and decide to not let them run your life

2. Focus again on breathing from the heart. Bring to your memory a person or a situation where you felt loved and respected. Experience those emotions again, right now, and surrender to the warm pleasant feeling this exercise generates. Let a smile come to your lips

3. Pay attention to the changes that are taking place in your body, your attitude and your perception. Enjoy that state of feeling loved and supported. **Ask your Heart to show you loving ways to take good care of yourself** and decide to behave accordingly.

Applications of Heart-Smiling to Personal Energy Management

Chapter 9

Taking Charge of your Energy

Taking charge of your energy is the ultimate self-empowerment choice. Freedom of choice is lost when someone merely reacts to neurotransmitter signals and allows them to run his or her life. Being aware of this process is the first step toward stopping this chemical hostile take over.

Neurotransmitters are what make us feel hungry, tired, bored or needy. Once aware of neurotransmitter signals, we can decide how to respond appropriately. The unaware can only react on instinct, which is not necessarily the healthy way.

Have you ever come home completely exhausted after a stressful day, with only one idea in mind, relax and do nothing? Then, the phone rings and a friend invites you to attend an activity you are gung-ho about. What happens to your energy level? Your brain sends you new messages via new neurotransmitters based on the information it received. Instantly, your level of energy surges. Suddenly, energy is abundant and excitement runs high.

This switch in the quality of energy happens because the brain sends out specific new neurotransmitters according to new information or new perception.

Heartfelt emotions like passion, love, friendship and purposefulness will stimulate human neurochemistry to improve energy levels.

Learning to choose a Lifestyle

Appropriately selected diet and exercises can address emotional/chemical imbalances, once one decides not to let neurotransmitters run ones life. Today, it is universally accepted that diet, exercise and supplements improve physical and mental health. Renowned author Dr. Dean Ornish[44] has extensively published material on these topics and advocates the benefits of low fat diet, exercises and spiritual practices. Dr. Michael Lesser[45] describes the foods and supplements that help balance brain chemistry in detail in his book, *"The Brain Chemistry Diet"*. Dr. John Gray[46], in his book *"Mars and Venus Diet and Exercise Solution"* lists foods and exercises for Mars (dopamine-driven) and Venus (serotonin-driven) personalities.

Applications of Heart-Smiling to Personal Energy Management

The "Food Lover" Life Style

Heart Smiling is especially aligned with a lifestyle that promotes good health and enjoyment of food. Practicing this Heart-centered technique helps one to choose *what type* of food is appropriate at each meal and *the best way* to enjoy it. "Food lovers" enjoy savoring the best foods and demand high quality and freshness. They take the time to develop a loving relationship with their food and their body.

A loving relationship with food requires time and care just like a relationship with a lover or friend. "Food lovers" enjoy everything about food. From planning to shopping for the perfect ingredients, they enjoy preparing their meals, and, of course, they take immense pleasure in savoring food slowly. The guiding principles of this approach are based on the love and respect ones heart has for ones body.

"Food Lover" Principles:

1. Love food and enjoy eating.
2. Eat only when hungry.
3. Do not eat when not hungry.
4. Create pleasant and peaceful surroundings when eating.
5. Savor each bite slowly.
6. Eat "live foods" like fruits and vegetables, dairy products (including whole milk, cream and butter), eggs, fish and meat.
7. Take "good" oils, like cold pressed olive oil and canola oil (rich in omega-3).
8. Limit sugar intake because sugar stimulates insulin production and creates cravings.
9. Avoid canned and bottled goods (additives, preservatives and other chemicals), as much as possible.
10. Appreciate, appreciate, and appreciate!

How one eats is as important as *what* one eats. The ultimate eating "sin" is rushing and stuffing. Eating slowly satisfies sooner. Rapid eating makes it impossible to evaluate the effect of each bite and almost always leads to an over-stuffed feeling.

Fast food is exactly what people do not need. It makes people fat not just because of the ingredients, but because it is fast! Fast food and TV dinners encourage stuffing and overeating. Eating in front of the television and not appreciating what is in ones' mouth is devastatingly unhealthy. Fast food is understandably banned from the food lover lifestyle.

Fat is not the enemy, *fast* is! There are two trends in fashionable dieting: "low-fat" or "low-carb" (carbohydrate). Supporters of each school of thought proselytize the benefits of their method and claim appealing results. The fact is that these diets have not been successful at making people healthier. North American statistics show an alarming increase in obesity and associated illnesses. It is time people start rethinking how they relate to food and begin using love as a principal ingredient.

Healthy food lovers adopt a lifestyle based on self-love and self-respect. They are not dieters. People who adopt the food lover lifestyle do not focus on avoiding types of nutrients like fat or carbohydrates, unlike those who do fashionable dieting. Rather, they focus on enjoying small portions of whatever their hearts desire.

 Follow your heart to self-love, health and happiness. Treating oneself with love is much healthier than treating oneself with fast food, even if it is low fat fast food. The main focus in ones life must become love, not being, efficient, on time and fast. Heart lovingly guides us to healthier thinner bodies.

In order to develop a love story with the food one eats, it is crucial to stop seeing food as a harmful substance that can make one sick or kill. Fat-phobia is pervasive in today's literature and thinking. Most people believe that fat causes heart disease. How can one assimilate with ease food that might kill them?

Western society's approach to dieting is not working. Fat may not be the "bad guy" after all. Statistics show a very low rate of obesity and heart diseases in Mediterranean countries where they eat cheese, cream, butter and olive oil on a daily basis.

Loving oneself enough to slow down, listen and trust the higher wisdom of the heart will be guided to a healthier and more enjoyable lifestyle. Luscious "triple crème" cheeses and Eggs Benedict can be part of ones diet. But, someone concerned about their weight must start looking from the viewpoint of self-love and conscious enjoyment, not reaction and habit.

Food Lovers Lifestyle Roadblocks

Personalities, according to their driving neurotransmitter, will have different difficulties in adopting the food lover's lifestyle.

1. Builders and Explorers: (adrenaline and dopamine-driven) have a tendency to eat too fast; food intake is often seen as a boring activity that takes time away from the serious issues. For these personality types, eating is something that needs to get done and over with as fast as possible, like putting gas in ones car. Builders and Explores will enjoy taking their time only after they learn to appreciate food. Self-respect will teach them to stop eating when they are not hungry, that is after learning to read brain signals of satisfaction when they have eaten enough.

2. Protectors: (serotonin-driven) tend to use food to regulate mood. They find it difficult to know the difference between "real" hunger and emotional hunger. Sugar is a problem for serotonin-driven persons because it tends to behave like an addictive substance for their brain. Eating sweets makes Protectors feel comfortable. During withdrawal, however, the lack of sugar makes them have cravings and mood swings. Protectors are more sensitive than others to carbohydrates. Practicing Heart Smiling helps Protectors learn to eat appropriate foods and manage emotions in a healthy way.

Food Supplements

A multiple vitamin rich in B complex, C and E, folic acid, calcium and magnesium on a daily basis is recommended to supplement everyone's diet. Our soils have long been depleted of these elements.

In addition, in order to keep heart cells and neurons healthy, one must provide the right nutrients that keep the cell membranes supple and permeable to chemical exchanges. This is especially crucial for heart-brain communication. Rigid neuron and heart cell membranes have been identified as responsible for many cardiac and mental disorders.

Omega-3 Fatty Acids

The role of omega-3 fatty acids has been recently studied by the medical community for its ability to restore cell membranes elasticity. Omega-3 oils have been shown to reduce symptoms of depression and other mood disorders[4]. Omega-3 fatty acids are now recommended for treatment and prevention of both post-heart attack and post-stroke depression.

Applications of Heart-Smiling to Personal Energy Management

Heart Smiling practitioners often take omega-3 fatty acids, because they know the importance of good quality heart and brain cell membranes for a successful heart-brain synchronization.

Tryptophane

The amino acid Tryptophane is a building block of serotonin and can be taken to help replenish Tryptophane deficiencies. In many countries, pure serotonin is not available, but can be bought as 5-HTP (5-hydroxy-tryptophne), its direct precursor (see fig. 31).

Tryptophane or 5-HTP can also help control appetite, especially for those who have a tendency to crave "comfort food" which can be a threat to a weight management program[5]. Protectors can benefit from taking this supplement on a daily basis to help control mood and cravings. Builders and Explorers can take tryptophane at bedtime to help induce sleep when they are too "hyper".

Choosing the right type of exercises

What is important about exercising is regularity and consistency, not intensity. 20 to 30 minutes of regular exercise, three times a week, increases endorphins in the blood, activates the parasympathetic system and sets the stage for enhancing cardiac coherence.

1. **Builders and Explorers** benefit from a more intensive exercise program like running, swimming, "cycling", and playing racquet sports, etc. for a period of 30 to 60 minutes at least three times a week. This intensity is needed to balance adrenaline and dopamine levels.

Taking Charge of your Energy

2. **Protectors** on the other hand, benefit from a moderate daily exercise program of 20 to 30 minutes. Long walks in nature, low-impact aerobics, slow jogging, stretching, aqua form, yoga, bicycle rides, skating and dancing are among the exercises they enjoy.

The goal of these exercises is to increase well-being, in the short and long term. Increased well-being starts right after exercising, while taking a shower. Overdoing is missing the point. Overdoing doesn't result in feeling good and puts the exerciser in risk of accidents. Over doers are more likely than not to give up and stop exercising after only a few sessions.

In order for an exercise program to support ones brain chemistry, one must exercise according to ones personality. Regular exercise helps decrease anxiety and depression.

Choose an enjoyable activity, start slowly and increase progressively. If possible, add invigorating music and link up with friends at the same level of endurance.

Weight management

Weight management is much easier when guided by heart wisdom. When one chooses eating habits and an exercise program in alignment with personality and brain chemistry, weight loss can be accomplished without starvation and deprivation.

In order to lose weight, there must be a negative balance between caloric intake and output. Serotonin-driven persons, whose recommended exercises burn fewer calories, must restrict caloric intake by eating smaller portions. Dopamine and adrenaline-driven persons can eat more calories.

As exercises recommended to serotonin-driven persons do not burn a lot of calories, Protectors trying to loose weight are sometimes tempted to select an exercise program that would burn more calories. Doing this jeopardizes neurochemical balance and mental well-being. Intense exercises will leave a serotonin-driven person exhausted, empty and in a bad mood. Exercises are supposed to give energy and put one in a good mood. If the exercise program you have chosen does not do that, choose again!

Dancing is an exercise worth considering, it energizes body and soul.
World champions
Billy Fajardo
Katie Marlow

Compulsive eating

Compulsive eaters keep eating despite the negative consequences and eat unhealthy foods. Diabetics, for example, who eat sweets or people with high cholesterol levels who eat fatty meats fall under this category. People who cannot chose the right food for them are at risk of becoming **food addicts**. Addicts are by definition people with inability to control the consumption of a substance, in this case food.

Neurotransmitters are released when one eats and create a sensation of pleasure, safety, plenty and satisfaction. Food addicts are not satisfied in the same manner as the rest of the population. A food addict's brain does not register feelings of satisfaction after eating small amounts of food. Their normal mechanisms of satisfaction have been disturbed. Food addicts who get comfort from food end up eating large quantities of "comfort food" in order to feel good.

"Comfort foods" are formulated to trigger the secretion of neurotransmitters that make people in an unbalanced emotional state feel good, often leading to addiction. After a food binge, food addicts feel sick, helpless and ashamed. They repeat this unhealthy behavior over and over again because the ability to choose what to eat is being controlled by brain chemistry and neurotransmitters.

Unlike alcohol or drug addiction, the goal of food addiction recovery cannot be abstinence. Alcohol and drugs can be avoided for the rest of ones life, but not food. Food addiction recovery is about regaining the ability to choose what to eat and when to eat.

Applications of Heart-Smiling to Personal Energy Management

Finding a health-supporting substitute for unhealthy self-destructing activity is currently the most widely used relapse prevention technique. The goal of substitution therapy is to replace a destructive behavior with a loving one. Alcoholics, for example, can learn self-respect by attending AA meetings instead of giving in to an urge to drink. But, what can a food addict do instead of eating when the urge is triggered? What loving activity could the addict engage in, that would produce the comfort that food provides? Each food addict has to find substitutes that fit their personality and preferences.

Ultimately, however, food addicts need to learn to love and respect themselves in order to overcome the need to feel good by abusing food. Self-love is at the core of recovery of all addiction. Self-love is the only emotion powerful enough to displace shame, fear and low self-esteem.

Heart-Smiling harnesses the power of self-love by allowing one to tap into the source of infinite love. Answers must not be sought outside self. Relaxing the need for food as a source of comfort by practicing Heart Smiling will change ones relationship with food.

Control of choice is regained through the higher energy and wisdom of the heart. Heart-Smiling guides one to the food and exercises that support health, satisfaction, ideal weigh and full energy capacity.

Taking Charge of your Energy

Heart-Smiling: Love-Powered Weight Management

1. Bring your attention to your heart and breathe effortlessly from the center of your chest. Become aware of your thoughts, feelings and sensations. Scan your body for any discomfort. Identify your energy type and the most prevalent neurotransmitter. Realize that your neurotransmitters are sending you messages that may not be supporting you intention to be healthy and thin.

2. Focus again on breathing from your heart. Bring to your awareness a memory of a situation where you experienced feeling loved and respected. Experience those emotions now and surrender to the warm fulfilling heart energy. Feel the healing power of this loving energy that can set you free from compulsive eating. Let a **smile** come to your lips.

3. Pay attention to the changes that are taking place in your body, your attitude and your perception.. While under the influence of this new loving self-perception, ask your heart to show you the foods and exercises that best support your weight management program. Be determined to lovingly follow through.

Neurotransmitters and Attitudes

Perception shapes experience and attitudes influence the way we experience life. Attitudes, like optimism, trust or cynicism are determined partly by neurotransmitters and genetics, and partly by past experience.

Optimists, for example, have a positive worldview and look forward to a better future. This attitude is both innate and acquired. Some people are born with enviable natural optimism.

In his book *"Learned Optimism"*, M. Seligman[6] affirms that those who are not born that way can learn to be optimistic. He describes persistence and hope as the two essential ingredients to an optimistic attitude. Persistence is a Builder (adrenaline-driven) attribute. Hope, on the other hand, is learned through previous successes and confidence that successes can be reproduced. M. Seligman illustrates the learning process of optimism using the example of laboratory animals.

> *A first group of animals had to push on a lever once in order to get food, and every time they would do so, food would come. If the mechanism was blocked so that food did not come when they pressed the lever, the animals got discouraged quickly and stopped pushing after 3 to 5 trials.*
>
> *A second group of animals had a different apparatus; the number of time they had to push the lever in order to get food was random. When their mechanism was blocked, there were ready to push on the lever many dozens of times before they abandoned the process: they were still hopeful.*

Optimism, the ability to believe in a better future, can be learned by addressing hope and the capacity to create new outcomes. M. Seligman teaches his patients to change the perception they have of their ability to intervene and modify reality. One must learn to see differently and believe one has the power to create a brighter future, regardless of past experience.

Heart-Smiling can teach pessimists to believe that good things can happen as a result of their own efforts and that difficult experiences are due to circumstance, thereby creating hope for a better future. Heart-Smiling changes self-perception and increases optimism.

Heart-Smiling: Boosting Optimism

1. Bring your attention to your heart and breathe effortlessly from the center of your chest. Become aware of your thoughts, feelings and sensations. Scan your body for any discomfort.

2. Focus again on breathing from your heart. Picture a situation, real or imagined, where you feel good about your accomplishments. Experience feeling **proud and self-confident.** Surrender to the warm heart energy filling your chest area. Let a **smile** come to your lips.

3. Pay attention to the changes that are taking place in your **posture**, your attitude and your perception. Ask Heart to let you **trust.** Decide to be open to the possibility of a bright and promising future and go forth with a spirit of **enthusiasm, excitement and expectancy.**

Neurotransmitters and Stress Management

Countless studies have shown an undeniable link between mental attitude, emotional reactions and long-term physical consequences. Studies on the psycho physiological effects of stress are irrefutable. Here are a few interesting research results in this area:

♦ A Harvard Medical School Study of 1,623 heart attack survivors found that when subjects became angry during emotional conflicts, their risk of subsequent heart attacks was more than double that of those that remained calm[50].

♦ Men who complain of high anxiety are up to six times more likely than calmer men to suffer sudden cardiac death[51].

♦ According to a Mayo Clinic study of individuals with heart disease, psychological stress was the strongest predictor of future cardiac events, such as cardiac death, cardiac arrest and heart attacks[52].

♦ In a study of 5,716 middle-aged people, those with the highest self-regulation abilities were over 50 times more likely to be alive and without chronic disease 15 years later than those with the lowest self-regulation scores[53].

♦ A recent study of heart attack survivors showed that patients' emotional state and relationships in the period after myocardial infarction are as important as the disease severity in determining their prognosis[54].

Participating in a stress management program helps correct adrenaline overproduction associated with stress. Stress produces devastating effects on blood vessels, on the immune system and on many organs.

The research on the effect of chronic stress in Dr. Hans Selye[55] laboratory animals showed that stressed animals die prematurely of cardiovascular diseases.

Stress Management is part of an Energy Management program, which teaches to avoid leaking energy in stressful situations, and to replenish energy through relaxation and meditation. These techniques bring deep relief to stress-related symptoms. Heart-Smiling, a form of introspective "open meditation", produces all the benefits of stress reducing techniques and has the advantage of being short and available at any moment.

Heart-Smiling: Instant Stress Management

1. Bring your attention to your heart and breathe effortlessly from the center of your chest. Become aware of your thoughts, feelings and sensations; identify any discomfort.

2. Focus again on breathing from your heart. Remember a situation where you felt calm, centered and relaxed. Experience those emotions again, and surrender to the warm heart energy filling you. Invite **peace and joy** in your hear. Let a **smile** come to your lips.

3. Pay attention to the changes that are taking place in your body, your attitude and your perception. **Appreciate the relaxed state** that is filling your body and keep smiling. Take advantage of this heart connection to ask your heart to maintain this state of peace, calm, joy and centeredness as long as you wish.

Neurotransmitters, Depression and Anxiety

Depression (often linked to serotonin dysfunction) and anxiety (related to Adrenaline and GABA imbalance) are disorders directly related to brain chemistry imbalance.

While co-director of the Complementary Medicine Center at University of Pittsburgh, neuropsychiatrist Dr David Servan-Scheiber[13] defined a strict alternative treatment protocol for depression and anxiety. Cardiac coherence techniques, physical activity, emotional communication skills, acupuncture and omega-3 oils are some of the approaches he studied that were shown to be effective in treating depression, stress and anxiety.

Pets for depressed patients were also recommended, for dogs and cats are known to be "men's best therapist". Animals are sensitive and have the ability to read human energy fields. Pets have been shown to be useful in stress, anxiety and depression reduction in many studies. Pets trigger feelings of unconditional love and offer an opportunity for humans to express heart-felt emotions. When petting them, our levels of endorphins rise from tactile pleasure.

Pets have the ability to open up hearts.

Heart-Smiling, using the superior emotions of the heart, can help people balance their brain chemistry and feel better.

> **Heart-Smiling: Soothing Depression or Anxiety**
>
> **1. Bring your attention to your heart and breathe effortlessly from the center of your chest.** Become aware of your thoughts, feelings and sensations; identify any discomfort. Realize that your **unbalanced neurotransmitters** are masking your underlying personality and robbing you of the energized life you deserve.
>
> **2. Focus again on breathing from your heart.** Remember a situation where you experienced feeling loved and valuable. Take advantage of this heart connection to feel the Universal Life Force energizing you and loving you. Let a **smile** come to your lips.
>
> **3. Pay attention to the changes** that are taking place in your body, your attitude and your perception. Ask your heart to guide you to recover your normal healthy level of neurotransmitters and energy. Determine to treat yourself with the love and respect.

Conclusion

Engaging your Heart

Using the Power of Heart-Smiling

Learning to manage personal energy is essential to the fully enjoy life. Heart-Smiling has the ability to engage the powerful energies of the heart and switch from a fear-based mindscape to a love-driven way of life.

The rewards of engaging our heart come with practice. Like any other technique, the more we practices Heart Smiling, the better we becomes at achieving life-changing results.

This technique offers a complementary approach to the treatment of many disorders, like addiction, stress reduction, depression reduction, anxiety reduction, weight management and any disorder where traditional western medicine is limited. Heart Smiling facilitates self-knowledge, self-love and self-respect, the prerequisites to a successful life. Only after knowing and loving ourself as Universal-Self can we start knowing and loving others.

Heart-Smiling has the power to alter perception, change attitudes, improve communication, promote bonding and transform lives. It fosters self-actualization and sustains planetary evolution.

Heart-Smiling is the ideal tool to manage all levels of personal energy because it taps into the feelings of being loved, safe, guided and protected, which are centered in our heart. People do not feel threatened and will easily drop conditioned defense mechanisms when in this loving state of heart connectedness.

Heart-based confidence will develop, as well as the power and courage to be vulnerable. Learning to access and manage our unlimited heart energy teaches us to stop giving power away by blaming or controlling. When we control our ability to change our mindscape, we have the power to transform our experience.

Heart-Smiling is the key that opens the doors to a rich and purposeful life, centered in peace, joy, power and love.

Engaging your Heart

Like John Lennon, I invite you to *"Imagine..."*

... *Imagine* yourself, your family, your workplace, your community, your city, your country, and the whole planet ...

... *Imagine* what it would be like if everyone was synchronizing their hearts and brains in joy, peace, gratitude and compassion.

... *Imagine* a smiling planet...

Engage your Heart and smile! And believe that this powerful loving energy in your heart can disarm and melt away all the fear and unhappiness on the entire planet.

This is the vision I share with you: a contagious smile that bonds all human hearts in peace, joy, gratitude and love.

With Gandhi, Mother Theresa and Martin Luther King, let us dream together the end of human suffering. As Heart-Smilers, we connect, radiate our healing heart energies, and bring forth the next phase of human evolution, the Age of Wisdom.

Mother Teresa of Calcutta

A smile from the Heart can heal anything.

"The day will come when, after harnessing space, the winds, the tides and gravitation, we shall harness for God the energies of love. And on that day, for the second time in the history of the world, we shall have discovered fire."
                                        Pierre Teilhard de Chardin

Table of Heart-Smiling Applications

The 3 steps of Heart-Smiling	61
Tap into the Power of Self-Love and Increase **Physical Energy**	96
Balance your **Sexual Energy**	101
Redirect your **Emotional Energy** from Fear to Love	114
Intellectual Energy and Wise Decision-Making	122
Foster **Personal Growth** and Find Your **Life Purpose**	125
Personal Leadership: Identify your driving Values	132
Serving a Higher Purpose	134
Self-Love for **Addicts & Co-Dependents**	177
Love-Powered **Weight Management**	189
Boosting **Optimism**	191
Instant **Stress Management**	193
Soothing **Depression or Anxiety**	195

Index

A
addiction   171, 172, 173, 176
addicts   177
adrenaline   159, 161, 163, 167, 175
anxiety   194, 195
attitudes   190

B
Builders   160, 163, 175, 182, 185

C
co-dependents   177
cocaine   164
compulsive eating   187
consciousness   141, 142, 146
cosmology   139

D
denial   172
depression   165, 194, 195
dopamine   158, 161, 164, 175

E
endorphins   166, 167
exercises   184
Explorers   160, 164, 175, 182, 185

F
"Food Lover" Life Style   180

G
GABA   166
gambling   173

I
illusion   142, 145, 146
Innocence   170
interpretation   144

M
meditation   193
mission   148

N
neurons 154
neurotransmitter 154, 157, 168, 171, 174, 178, 187, 190, 194
nicotine addiction 175

O
omega-3 fatty 183
optimism 191

P
passion 179
perception 171, 177, 178
photon 142, 151
Protectors 160, 165, 175, 183, 185, 186

Q
quantum soup 141, 151

R
reality 138, 142, 144, 169

S
Self-love 188
separation 149
serotonin 159, 161, 165, 167, 175
singularity 139
smiling planet 198
stress management 192, 193

T
transcendence 146, 148, 150
tryptophane 184

U
Universal Love 148, 150

W
weight management 186, 189
Wise-Innocent 170

References

[1] Gibran, Kahlil (1990): *Spirits Rebellious*, Citadel Press, New York

[2] Emerson, Ralph Waldo (1926): *Emerson's Essays*, Harper & Row, New York

[3] MacFerland, B.H. et al. (1985) *Utilization patterns among long term enrollees in pre-paid group practice health maintenance organization,* Medical Care 23: 1121-1233

[4] Pharmacy Times (2002) *Top 10 drugs of 2001,* Vol. 68(4): 10-15

[5] Servan-Schreiber, D., W.M. Perlstein, et al. (1998). *Selective pharmacological activation of limbic structures in human volunteers: A positron emission tomography study.* Journal of Neuropsychiatry and Clinical Neurosciences **10**: 148-59

[6] Goleman, Daniel (1995): *"Emotional Intelligence"* Bantam, New York

[7] Cantin, M. et Genest, J (1986) *The heart as an endocrine gland* Clinical and Investigating Medicine **9**(4): 319-327

[8] Armour, J.A and Ardell, J. (1994) *"Neurocardiologie"* Oxford Press

[9] McCraty, R., M. Atkinson, et al. (1995). *The effects of emotions on short term heart rate variability using power spectrum analysis.* American Journal of Cardiology 76: 1089-1093.

[10] **Institute of HeartMath**, located in Boulder Creek, California, is a non-profit research and education organization dedicated to the development and implementation of positive emotion-refocusing tools.

[11] McCraty, R. and A. Watkins (1996). *Autonomic Assessment Report: A Comprehensive Heart Rate Variability Analysis – Interpretatio nGuide and Instructions.* Boulder Creek, CA, Institute of HeartMath.

[12] Rein, G., M. Atkinson, et al. (1995). *The physiological and psychological effects of compassion and anger.* Journal of Advancement in Medicine 8(2): 87-105.

[13] McCraty, R. (2000). *Psychophysiological coherence: A link between positive emotions, stress reduction, performance and health.* Proceedings of the Eleventh International Congress on Stress, Hawaii.

[14] For more information on biofeedback software "Freeze Framer" go to **www.heartmath.com**

[15] Tiller, W., R. McCraty, et al. (1996). *Cardiac coherence; A new non-invasive measure of autonomic system order.* Alternative Therapies in Health and Medicine 2(1): 52-65.

[16] McCraty, R., M. Atkinson, et al. (1996). *The Electricity of Touch: Detection and measurement of cardiac energy exchange between people.* Proceedings of the Fifth Appalachian Conference on Neurobehavioral Dynamics: Brain and Values, Radford VA

[17] McCraty, R., B. Barrios-Choplin, et al. (1998). *The impact of a new emotional self-management program on stress, emotions, heart rate variability, DHEA and cortisol.* Integrative Physiological and Behavioral Science 33(2): 151-170

[18] *"Maximizing performance while reducing risk"*. HeartMath Research Center, Institute of HeartMath, Publication No. 00-11. Boulder Creek, CA, 2000.

[19] Rollin McCraty, PhD, Mike Atkinson and Lee Lipsenthal, MD. Submitted to Diabetic Medicine.

[20] Frederic Luskin, PhD, Thomas Gregory Quinn, MD, et al. Abstract in: Journal of Cardiopulmonary Rehabilitation. 2000; 20 (5): 303.

[21] Deborah Rozman, PhD, Rupert Whitaker, PhD, et al. Complementary Therapies in Medicine. 1996; 4 (4): 226-232.

[22] Bob Barrios-Choplin, PhD, Rollin McCraty, PhD and Bruce Cryer, MA. Stress Medicine. 1997; 13 (3): 193-201.

[23] Bob Barrios Choplin, PhD, Rollin McCraty, PhD, Joseph Sundram, MEd and Mike Atkinson *The effect of employee self-management training on personal and organizational quality.* HeartMath Research Center, Institute of HeartMath, Publication No. 99-083. Boulder Creek, CA, 1999.

[24] Rollin McCraty, PhD, Dana Tomasino, BA, Mike Atkinson and Joseph Sundram, MEd. HeartMath Research Center, Institute of HeartMath, Publication No. 99-075. Boulder Creek, CA,1999.

[25] Rollin McCraty, PhD, Mike Atkinson, Dana Tomasino, BA, Jeff Goelitz, MEd and Harvey N. Mayrovitz, MD. Integrative Physiological and Behavioral Science. 1999; 34 (4): 246-248.

[26] Collaborative study conducted by the Institute of HeartMath, Pam Aasen, PhD and Stephanie J. Thurik, MEd. HeartMath Research Center, Institute of HeartMath, Publication No. 00-10. Boulder Creek, CA, 2000.

[27] Frederic Luskin, PhD, MFCC. PhD Dissertation, Counseling Psychology, Stanford University.

[28] Bowly, John (1969) *"Attachment and Loss Vol. I. Attachment."* Penguin, London, England

[29] Piaget, Jean (1957) *"Construction of reality in the child"* Routledge, London

[30] Spitz, Rene (1939) Early bounding and attachment studies

[31] Duchenne de Boulogne *"The Mechanisms of Human Facial Expression"*, first published in French in 1862

[32] Ekman, P & Rosenberg, E.L. (1997) *"What the face reveals. Basic and applied studies of spontaneous expression using the facial action coding system"*. Oxford University Press, New York

[33] Maslow, Abraham (1964): *"Toward a Psychology of Being"* Van Nostrand, Princeton

[34] Barrett, Richard (1998) *"Liberating the Corporate Soul"* Butterworth-Heinemann

[35] Redfield, James (1997) *"Celestine Prophecy"* Warner Books

[36] Cirulnik, Boris (1999): *"Le Merveilleux Malheur"* Odile Jacob, Paris

Cirulnik, Boris (2001): *"Les vilians petits canards"* Odile Jacob, Paris

[37] Joseph Chilton Pearce (2002) *"The Biology of Transcendence"* Park Street Press, Rochester, Vermont

[38] Chopra, Deepak (1990): *"Ageless Body, Timeless Mind"* Harmony Books, New York

[39] Davies, Paul (1983) : *"God & the New Physics"* Simon & Schuster, New York

[40] Lederman, Leon (1993) : *"The God Particle"* Delta, New York

[41] Goswami, Amit (1993): *"The Self-Aware Universe"* Tarcher/Putman, New york

[42] Russell, Peter (2003) : *"From science to God"* New World Library, Novato, CA

[43] Black, Claudia (1982): *"It Will Never Happen to Me."* MAC Publishing, Denver CO

[44] Ornish, Dean MD (1983): *"Stress, Diet and your Heart"* Putman, New York

Ornish, Dean (1990): *"Program for reversing heart disease"* Random House, New York

[45] Lesser, Michael (2002): *"The Brain Chemistry Diet"* Putman, New York

[46] Gray, John (2003): *"The Mars & Venus diet and exercise solution"* St. Martin's Press, New York

[47] Stoll, A. L. (2001) *"The Omega-3 Connection: the ground-braking Omega-3 Antidepression Diet and Brain Program"*. Simon & Schuster, New York

[48] Seidan, Onthiel MD (founder of Doctors of the World) (1998) *"The serotonine connection"* Prima Health, Rocklin, CA

[49] Seligman, Martin (1991): *"Learned Optimism"* Knopf, New York

[50] M. Mittleman et al. (1995) Circulation.; 92(7)

[51] I. Kawachi et al. (1994) Circulation.; 89(5).

[52] T. Allison et al. (1995) Mayo Clin Proc.; 70(8)

[53] R. Grossarth-Maticek & H. Eysenck. (1995) Person Individ Diff.; 19(6)

[54] S. Thomas et al. (1997) Am J Crit Care.; 6(2)

[55] Selye, Hans (1955) "The physiology and Pathology of exposure to Stress" Montreal: Acecta

[56] Servan-Schreiber, David (2003) : *"Guérir le stress, l'anxiété et la dépression sans médicaments ni psychanalyse"* Ed : Robert Laffont

**GIVE THE GIFT OF THE ENERGIZING HEART
TO YOUR FRIENDS AND COLLEAGUES.**

Attention corporations, universities, colleges, professional and non-profit organizations: quantity discounts are available on bulk purchases.

Check your local Bookstore

or order online at www.YouAreEnergy.com

or call us at (954) 649-1413.

Heart-Smiling Workshops

Dr Campeau is dedicated to training groups and individuals who want to master the Heart-Smiling technique and reap the benefits of increased energy in their personal and professional lives.

Heart-Smiling workshops take participants through the four levels of Heart-Smiling practice: alone and in interaction with others; in calm, stressing or conflicting situations. Participants get acquainted with the physiology of heart-brain synchronization and learn to channel the powerful energies of their heart to increase personal energy in multiple everyday life situations.

More and more health professionals, teachers, managers and business owners use cardiac coherence inducing techniques to better manage their own energy and to help their patients, students and employees. Regular practice of Heart-Smiling energizes lives. This high energy also disseminates to those around, thus enhancing quality of life at home and at work.

You energy is precious. Learn to manage it efficiently by harnessing the power of your heart.

Do not hesitate to contact us for more information.
Visit our website: www.YouAreEnergy.com
Or call us at (954) 649-1413

Your Heart will set you free.